One
of the
Lucky Ones

A.E. LEE

Fulton Books
Meadville, PA

Published by Fulton Books 2022

ISBN 979-8-88505-281-8 (paperback)
ISBN 979-8-88505-282-5 (digital)

Printed in the United States of America

One day
You will tell your story
Of how you overcame
What you went through
And it will be
Someone else's
Survival guide

—Brene Brown

To my parents, thank you for always believing in me (regardless if it was my childhood aspiration to be Alice and Wonderland or a writer).

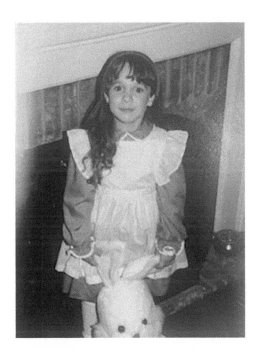

Contents

Preface...ix

Part 1

Chapter 1: Let's Start at the Very Beginning 3
Chapter 2: Red Flags are Meant to be Ignored, Right?..............8
Chapter 3: Band of Gold (or a Really Big Diamond Ring) 12
Chapter 4: Nowhere to Run 17
Chapter 5: And Baby Makes Three...Then Four!......................23
Chapter 6: Enough...31
Chapter 7: So There's This Hot Twenty-Four-Year-Old 34
Chapter 8: August 3, 2019 38

Part 2

Chapter 9: The Aftermath..47
Chapter 10: These are Going to be the Worst Days of My Life 51
Chapter 11: You Say Therapist, I Hear Psychic........................55
Chapter 12: London Calling 61
Chapter 13: Things can Always be Worse................................64
Chapter 14: The Mother-in-Law..68
Chapter 15: Things Got Worse... 73
Chapter 16: And Then, He Cheated 78
Chapter 17: Holy Crap, I'm Pregnant!...................................81
Chapter 18: Rock-Bottom..85
Chapter 19: Still Standing...a Conclusion of Sorts....................90

Acknowledgments 95

Preface

*I always liked the word preface better
than foreword; sounds fancier.*

—A.E. Lee

EVERY AUTHOR I HAVE EVER read has said that their book was a labor of love. This was so much more; this was therapy. Writing this is what I turned to when I felt like I had hit rock bottom.

I have been told, as I am sure you have before, writing is therapeutic. I was resistant, however. When I was younger, I attempted to journal or keep a diary but with little success. I would go to Barnes and Noble, buy the prettiest journal, and dream of sitting under a tree and writing down my deepest, darkest secrets while pretending I was in some Jane Austen novel. Then, I would rush home, put pen to paper, and...nothing. I would get distracted, and eventually, the journal would end up in a junk drawer. I amassed quite the collection, and now, my five-year-old is enjoying all of them for her drawings.

It was not until my psychic (go ahead, roll your eyes) urged me to do something with the excess energy that was bottled up inside me. "You have got to do something. We tried knitting and that didn't work. Maybe write a book."

I laughed. Yeah, okay, sure, I'll write a book. I will squeeze that into my life as a single, working mom while going for my second master's degree. No problem.

But I actually did. I realized that maybe, just maybe, someone will read this and could be helped. Then, it will be worth it. My story is not a fairytale, and it is a reality that millions of women face every day. The only difference between me and many of them is that I got out.

I am a survivor of domestic violence. Even writing those words down now sends a chill up my spine. *Survivor of domestic violence.* I watch Lifetime, I've seen the afterschool specials, attended events in support of ending domestic violence. Hell, one of my favorite made-for-TV movies, *No One Would Tell* starring Candance Cameron Bure, is all about domestic violence.

The denial is what got me in the end. The denial that what I was experiencing day in and day out was domestic violence. The name-calling, the gaslighting, and even at times the physical violence. And I had seen what the survivors look like; I didn't look like them. I had the perfect Instagram family: handsome husband, two beautiful children, and a big beautiful house in the suburbs of Washington, DC. I am an intelligent woman, but to have to say out loud that I was being abused is still too much for me to handle.

As you read my story, please know that yes, it is all factual, and yes, my children and I are safe. I am one of the lucky ones. Not only was I able to get away, I had the financial means to fight. The unfortunate reality is that domestic violence victims stay with their abusers because of fear and not having anywhere else to turn.

As I said, this is no fairy tale. Every word that details what happened to me over the course of that ten-year period is my own, pen to paper. There are highs and there are extreme lows, and through it all, I tried to maintain a sense of humor—after all, laughter through tears is my most favorite emotion.

Part 1

Chapter 1:
Let's Start at the Very Beginning

Hold on, I think I need to pour
a glass of wine for this.
— Chris Lewis (my dear friend)

I HAVE ALWAYS LOVED THE MOVIE *27 Dresses*, which is the story of a hopeless romantic who is always a bridesmaid and never a bride and is just waiting for her turn to find true happiness. I could relate to it so well. I was ready for my chance—I wanted to get married and have children, something I had dreamed about since as long as I can remember. After buying my seventh bridesmaid's dress, I had about enough. I was also in a four-year, long distance relationship that was going nowhere. I tried desperately to convince my boyfriend that we should get married, but fortunately for both of us, he was smart enough to realize that we were wrong for each other. (Don't get me wrong, when he broke up with me three days before Christmas, I wanted to smash his face in, but I took a girls' trip to Vegas a few days later and that helped me forget about things).

After the breakup, I proceeded to unhappily date around for a few months. I dated a guy who had breathalyzer in his car (something my friends will never let me forget), dated someone who said they were separated and turned out to be very much still married (still feel bad about that one), and "dated" someone who could have been an underwear model (one of my proudest accomplishments to date). I was still very unhappy, and I was ready to get married and have children. I was trying to speed up time, which generally does not work out in my favor ever. Enter the ex, Don.

Don and I met at a house party in Philadelphia. I'm from the city of Brotherly Love (go ahead and sing the *Rocky* theme song or the theme song from *Fresh Prince*, I get it all the time), and he was living just outside of Washington, DC. His college roommate, Hugo, happened to be dating my work colleague, Laura, and they were throwing a party. Laura told me, "There would be a lot of single guys there," but as I walked into Hugo's townhouse in central Philly and scanned the crowd, I didn't see anyone I would be interested in.

As the drinks began to flow so did games of flip cup, and I began chatting with the people around me. Hugo introduced me to his friend, Don, who is not my usual type. He seemed well, nerdy. He had dark hair and glasses, and he was talking about the latest iPhone and Apple products. Then, he started going on and on about how he was half-Chinese and would be getting dim sum with his parents.

There was no initial spark, no fireworks. He seemed like a nice guy. We became Facebook friends, and honestly, I never thought I would see him again. Until one day in April.

I was sitting alone in my apartment, feeling very alone. It was a cozy one-bedroom apartment, French doors separating the bedroom from the living space. I loved that apartment and still do. It even had a washer and dryer in the unit, which was imperative back in the days that bars allowed smoking.

Don and I started messaging on Facebook; I cannot remember who messaged who first. I remember staring at my screen thinking, *just go for it.*

As I said, Don was not my typical type; however, my "type" did not seem to be working out so well for me. I messaged him and told him that we should see each other when he was in the Philadelphia area on an upcoming trip.

It was decided that he was going to come up one weekend in May, and we were going to hang out with Hugo and Laura. After the messages, I remember thinking, *what have I done?*

I immediately called Laura and told her. She said, "No, just no. He is geographically undesirable."

I heard her, loud and clear. The last thing I wanted to do was another long-distance relationship, yet here I was pursuing one. I still remember saying to her, "I hear you. Let's just see what happens. I mean, I've got nothing to lose."

We went out that weekend in May. The four of us ended up at a bar not far from Hugo's townhouse. The foursome trickled down to a threesome, then just a twosome. He was charming, and we talked and talked about everything. When we walked back to Hugo's, where we were both staying, Don held my hand. We ended up sharing a bed that night, and by the morning, I knew that this was someone I wanted to have a future with.

We began dating right away. It became serious pretty fast, with both of us splitting weekends of travel back and forth between Philadelphia and Washington. Everyone loved him; his family embraced me and mine did the same with him. My niece, who had made her feelings of dislike for my previous boyfriend very much known, gave her seal of approval and began picking out what fancy dress she would wear in our wedding.

I have to admit, I did too. Very quickly into the relationship, I realized that we both were ready to do what we had not in previous relationships: settle down and get married. It also became clear that traveling back and forth and sitting in I-95 traffic every weekend was not ideal for either of us.

At this point, I had decided that a career in politics was not for me. I had been working for a state representative for seven years, and the twenty-four-hour-on-call-with-little-pay was not how I wanted to spend any more of my life. I come from a family of teachers, and while I had played with the notion of possibly going into education, I wanted to do something different.

After year two of politics, my mother and my sister, Tara, sat me down and implored me to just try an education class at the community college. I did and I loved it. I was working on my degree in early childhood education when Don and I began dating. He quickly convinced me that I would never make any money being a daycare teacher and suggested I go for a master's degree in education instead.

He was very convincing, as was his father who told me on multiple occasions that I was stupid for not going for a master's degree.

Wanting to impress everyone, and still not quite sure what direction I wanted my life to go in, I applied to Marymount University in Virginia and got in. It was right down the street from Don, and we made a plan to move in together shortly after the one-year mark of our relationship.

You know that feeling you get in your gut? When you think you don't know if you should do something? I get it every time I get onto an airplane. I am deathly afraid of flying—actually scratch that—I'm scared of crashing. I fly frequently, but I still have that feeling.

And that was the feeling I had when we decided I was going to move to Virginia that following December and to start school. I wonder now, looking back, what would have happened if I had trusted my gut.

My friend Joe, sensing my growing trepidation as the move date approached, took me out to a wine bar to talk some sense into me. Joe and I met years prior when he was working for a neighboring state representative, and he is that one friend that everyone has who can bridge the gap between being supportive and tough love all at the same time. He is, still to this day, the best thing that I ever got from my short-lived career in politics.

He said to me that night, "Reeder (my maiden name, which he still calls me), I love you and I support whatever decision you make. But are you sure you want to do this?"

"Yes. I love him. I am ready for this next step. I want to do this. I need to get out of Philadelphia and do something different," I said.

"I know and I support that. Just, are you sure it should be with him?" I will never forget the look in Joe's eyes. I thought at the time he needed reassurance that I knew what I was doing and that I was going to be okay. Looking back now, I realize he was pleading with me to change my mind.

"I'm good, honestly. I know what I am doing," I said to Joe, trying to convey a look of confidence that I did in fact know what I was doing. In reality, I was not so sure.

We had been fighting a lot and not just a disagreement here and there. These fights were loud screaming matches, normally with cursing and name-calling and me trying to match Don's yelling. I had never experienced anything like this before. I told myself that these loud, explosive fights just meant we had a lot of passion between us. We always made up, and he always said he was sorry and that he loved me. I was sure that other people had arguments just like this but just didn't talk about it. I was convinced that these fights were just growing pains. We had to learn how to communicate, and we were just on the cusp of a huge life change.

In December 2011, I moved down to Virginia to be with Don. It took me exactly eleven minutes to realize I had just made the biggest mistake of my life.

Chapter 2:
Red Flags are Meant to be Ignored, Right?

The same red flags you ignore in the beginning
will be the same reason it all ends.

—Unknown

I REMEMBER MEETING DON'S FRIENDS AT the beginning of our relationship. All of the women would make comments to me about his anger:

"He's great, but he definitely has an anger problem."

"Have you seen his temper yet?"

"There was this one time I thought we were going to have to call the police. He was so mad at his brother."

Looking back, I wish I could shake myself. Why did I think hearing this was normal? I laughed it off. They must be mistaken; he doesn't have an anger problem. I'm a smart woman, I would have seen evidence of an anger problem if there was one.

I did get up the guts to ask him about it one day. Why were all his friends, and his parents at times, talking about his temper? He said, "Yeah, I used to have a real anger problem, but I've learned to control my temper."

"That's great, did you go to anger management or do therapy?" I asked, thinking what a forward-thinking boyfriend I had for recognizing he had a problem and getting help on his own.

"No. I just learned how to control it."

Right. Okay, so maybe not as forward-thinking as I initially thought. Still, he had learned to control his anger and besides the occasional fight (*occasional* would be a loose term here; it was often and explosive, but I was still in the denial phase), I had not seen the anger.

I remember where I was standing the first moment, he truly yelled at me and unleashed his temper. I remember where I was every time he yelled at or hit me, but the first time hit me hard. The anger I tried so hard not to see suddenly appeared inches from my face, wearing a white trash costume.

It was Halloween, and we were at his brother's house for a Halloween party with a bunch of friends—and by friends, I mean his friends. I learned early on that we would be spending most of our time with his friends, not mine. Not for any reason other than because he did most of the traveling up, he made the plans for us on the weekends—and I allowed him to do so.

That night, Don dressed as white trash and I was an '80s prom queen. The evening started out fun, with everyone in costumes ranging from Audrey Hepburn to Harry Potter. As the drinks started flowing, however, I could see the agitation growing across Don's face. Something was making him annoyed; I just could not put my finger on what it was.

We began arguing, and I asked that we talk upstairs so that we could stop drawing so much attention to ourselves. He began yelling, and I tried to match his yelling, which just infuriated him more. He grabbed my arms, tight and hard. Nose-to-nose with me and within centimeters of my face, he yelled, "You cunt, now I am really mad. You wanted to see what me angry looked like, here it is, you stupid bitch!"

Then, he walked out.

I was stunned and didn't know what to do. I sat on the bed crying. What the hell had just happened? His friend Suzie came in, trailed by Lori, his brother's girlfriend at the time. Both of them tried to calm me down and reassure me.

"He's yelled at me like that before too," Lori said.

"He has put me in tears so much from yelling at me I can't even remember," Suzie said. "It will be okay. I mean, if you are going to be with him, you were bound to see the anger at some point."

Again, what the hell was going on? I just got screamed at, grabbed at, and called the c-word by a person who supposedly loves me. Now, I am being comforted by two women I barely know, basically telling me this was normal behavior for him.

I knew this was not normal, and I knew I did not want to feel like this. I called Joe.

"Where are you? I'm coming to get you," Joe said.

I had someone ready to come and rescue me, and then, I had people telling me that this was all normal. I knew this was not right, but I also knew I did not want to leave. Something was preventing me from leaving—was it fear or something else?

Don walked in and with tears in his eyes, begged for my forgiveness. Apologized profusely. Told me it would never happen again. Begged me not to leave, not to leave him. He told me that if I wanted him to, he would get professional help. He promised me again it would never happen again. I believed him. I should not have.

The fighting continued. It was not constant—it ebbed and flowed—but it continued.

A few weeks before I left for Virginia, while out with friends, we had another explosive fight right in the middle of South Street in downtown Philly. We began fighting because Don had accused me of flirting with our friend, Blair. Blair and Don had been friends for years, and he quickly became my friend too. At times, he seemed to be my only ally.

This fight, Don kept the insults to just the two of us. He texted them to me.

"You stupid cunt. I can't believe you would flirt with him."

"You are such an embarrassment. You are worthless."

"Good. Leave. You aren't worth it anyway," Don texted.

Tears and tears just streamed down my face. How could this be happening again? He said this would never happen and it is, with just a few weeks left before we are set to move in together. What am

I going to tell everyone? I was so ready for this to be it, but I knew I did not want it to feel like this.

Don's friends (who we were out with again) scooped me up and dropped me off at my apartment. Don was waiting for me, apologizing, and swearing that he would never do it again. He was going to get professional help. He texted all of our friends that were out with us and apologized to them for what they had witnessed. I believed him again, and again, I should not have.

Chapter 3:
Band of Gold (or a Really Big Diamond Ring)

I've been dating since I was fifteen.
I'm exhausted. Where is he?
—Kristin Davis, *Sex and the City*

WE MOVED IN TOGETHER IN December and were engaged in June. It was supposed to be a magical proposal, and I absolutely knew it was coming; I had snooped. I told him I always wanted to wear my grandmother's engagement ring, a solitaire three-carat diamond on a platinum band. I had checked my parent's safe the weekend before while we were visiting, and it was not there. I knew he had it and that an engagement was coming.

I had gone on a business trip with him to San Francisco. We were at the Top of the Mark, with its sweeping views of the city. It was a rare clear day, and you could see every part of San Francisco. We were seated at a corner table, the best in the place for drinks, and then, we were going to have dinner at a fancy restaurant in the city. I had bought a new dress at Nordstrom's for the occasion, brilliant purple with cap sleeves. I figured you only get engaged once—why not splurge on a new dress? (At least that is what I told myself.) Don looked handsome in a suit. We were the picture-perfect couple, and both of us were nervous about what was about to unfold.

Since it was the best table, people kept coming up to take their pictures right by our table. A group of women, who had clearly had a few drinks already, came up to get their picture taken. One of them

12

knocked into Don's chair. She apologized and then said, "Sorry for interrupting your romantic date. Now, don't go getting engaged!"

I am a firm believer in signs. This was a sign—it was either a sign we should not be getting engaged or a sign that I was wrong and this was not going to happen. But it did happen. He downed his martini and asked me to marry him. It took me a minute to realize what was going on, and then, I said yes. He pulled out the ring, the ring I had imagined on my finger since my grandmother passed fifteen years prior.

I should back up a minute and explain the importance of the ring. My grandmother was the most amazing woman I have ever met, and I am so fortunate to have had her in my life for fifteen years. I wanted to be as magnetic of a person as I remembered her being. I recall, as a little girl, looking through all of her jewelry and pretending it was mine. Everything sparkled, and when she put on a piece and smiled at me, she lit up the room.

I particularly loved her ring—the engagement ring my grandfather put on her finger. It was beautiful, and I will always remember the way it sparkled in the sunlight when we would take our walks together. The diamond has been in my family for over one hundred years, and when she lost her battle with lung cancer, the ring was given to my mother. I started my campaign right there and then to have it when it was my turn to get married.

I cried when he put the ring on my finger. I felt like I had a piece of my grandmother back with me, a piece I had been longing for since that awful day in January. And then reality set in—holy crap, I was engaged! I had done it. It was my turn. I was finally going to be a bride and not a bridesmaid. I was going to get married and have children. My "dream" was coming true.

I woke up the next morning before Don. I lay in my hotel bed, just staring at the ring on my finger. Why, if I had everything I had ever wanted, did I feel like something was amiss? It was that same gut feeling, telling me something was wrong. So I did what I normally did when it came to that feeling and Don: I shoved the feeling deep down and pressed on. I had my grandmother's ring, and I was going to get married. I was going to have the wedding of my dreams.

It took us about a week to start fighting again. We were headed back up to Philadelphia for an engagement party that my friends were throwing us. I was so excited to show off my ring and to celebrate with our friends; he was not. He was agitated, weaving in and out of traffic, and cutting cars off left and right. I yelled at him for scaring me, and he yelled at me for yelling at him.

We pulled into the Wawa by my parents' house. By now, I was crying…again. I begged him to act like he loved me in front of my parents and all our friends. He looked me straight in the eye and with absolutely no feeling, said, "I am very good at acting like I love you."

I cried harder, and he got more annoyed. I felt trapped, like I couldn't breathe. This was not right; I did not deserve to be treated like this. But I loved him, and he loved me, right? I had the ring I had always wanted, and I had started planning the wedding. If we broke up, what would I tell everyone? I would feel like such a fool.

So we pulled out of the Wawa parking lot, I pulled myself together, and by the time we showed up to my parent's house, we were ourselves. The epitome of a newly-engaged loved up couple.

The fighting was hitting an all-time high the weeks following the engagement. Perhaps it was the stress of the realization that we were getting married. Things reached a peak on a summer evening in August. A fight about something miniscule that turned into something major, and I had had enough. I was standing in the kitchen of our small apartment, fuming and trying to clean up from dinner. I was not going to take his verbal abuse anymore.

"Where's my wine?" Don yelled.

"I'm drinking it," I said.

He walked over slowly and while staring me in the eye, took the glass of wine from me and poured its contents over my head. As he walked away, I snapped and shoved him.

What followed felt like it was happening in slow motion. He turned around and looked at me with a look I had never seen before. His eyes went black, and right there and then, I thought he was going to kill me.

He headbutted me, backing me into the bedroom; it hurt like hell. I fell onto the bed and onto a pile of plastic from the dry cleaning that I had picked up earlier in the day. Once I hit the bed, he wrapped his hands around my neck. I begged him to stop, or at least I tried to do so, but words could not come out.

By some miracle, he let go and got off me. As I tried to run away, he shoved me into the wall, breaking one of my toes. When I collapsed on the floor, he taunted me, "What are you going to do, leave?"

I hid my face in my hands and just tried to imagine this awful experience ending.

"You know what, forget you. I'm leaving," he said as he slammed the door behind him.

I got up, ran to the door, and locked it, collapsing again to the floor. I found myself repeating the same phrases over and over again: what just happened? What am I doing? What do I do now?

I knew if I called my parents, siblings, or friends they would be in their car to come get me before we hung up. But I was not sure I wanted that. Looking back, that sounds crazy—this man just attacked me, why would I want to marry him still? It's a question I ask and have asked over and over again.

I ultimately called the only person I knew would not judge him or me. I called his mom, Helen, and told her what just happened. She listened and made sure I was safe. She called him to make sure he was safe and convinced him to come back. I let him in, and he slept on the couch.

The next morning, he went early to work. I was in grad school then and did not have class until noon. Helen called.

"I called my friend Hedy, and she said you can come stay with her anytime. I think you should keep a bag in your car with clothes in case you ever need to leave quickly. I do. And Amanda, I have to tell you, if you ever call me and tell me something like that again, if you don't call the police, I will."

I was in shock. On one hand, I felt like someone understood what I was going through. But on the other hand, my future mother-in-law just told me to keep a bag in my car for a quick getaway and that she was going to call the police on her son. What the hell was going on? I was so confused; I was confused about what happened and confused about what she had just told me.

Don called and asked me to meet him for lunch to talk. We met at a local restaurant by his office. I showed up without the engagement ring on. I took it off the night before, and I could not bring myself to put it back on. He noticed immediately.

We talked. Well, he talked. Apologized. Told me that he would get help and that we should get help as a couple before we got married. This was a new one. I am all for therapy and had previously seen a therapist for anxiety who had been a godsend. I said I would stay but only if we got help together.

I called what felt like a hundred therapists. No one who took our insurance was available during the times we were. As a newly engaged couple with only one of us working at the time, we were not in a position to pay someone out of pocket.

We never saw a therapist. I gave up, and things got better. I again tried to convince myself that this was all growing pains, and we were past it. I began to plan my dream wedding.

We were married on June 9, 2012. The night before, Don broke his hand in a fight at the hotel bar. In the words of Joe, "Well, if ever there was a sign, that sure was it."

I chose to ignore it.

It was the perfect wedding and the nicest wedding I have ever been to. I had everyone who meant something to me there, and the food, the flowers (daisies and peonies, my favorite), the cake (vanilla with raspberry cream in the middle), and the music were on point. I wore a beautiful A-line lace dress, and my hair and makeup were done by professionals for the first time. I had never felt so pretty, and I was ready for the fresh start, and that I was hoping this wedding would bring for both of us.

Chapter 4:
Nowhere to Run

I'm trapped in a glass case of emotion.
—Will Ferrell, *Anchorman*

"I FEEL DIFFERENT—DO YOU FEEL DIFFERENT? I feel more in love and grounded," Don told me. We were in a cab somewhere in Jamaica on the way to the luxury hotel that would be our home for a week.

"Yeah, absolutely," I replied. I didn't lie to him, exactly; I did feel different.

I felt trapped.

I felt like I had just made the biggest mistake of my life. What was I doing? While things had gotten better, we still fought a lot. The fighting was not kind, though I suppose kindness is not a part of most arguments. I still remember, as a little girl, hiding in the bathroom as my parents yelled at each other. That was not what I wanted for my future children, and I especially did not want my future children to hear their father call me awful names or say how stupid and worthless I was.

I sat in the hotel bathtub that night, thinking I had never felt so low. Maybe I *was* worthless, maybe his anger *was* my fault, and maybe if I just learned not to set him off, we could be happy.

I looked over to the mirror in the massive bathroom. I looked utterly drained. I had dark circles under my eyes, and despite my month of tanning before the wedding, I was very pale.

I felt like I had two choices. I could just end my life, which I knew was not an option for me as I could not bear to think of the hurt that would cause my parents, my siblings, and my nieces. The second was to grin and bear it. I had made my choice on June 9, 2012; I married him. I was his wife. I needed to try to make the best of this, and if I tried hard enough, he would love me and not hurt me anymore. At least, that is what I told myself.

It never even crossed my mind that just leaving him was an option.

I got out of the bathtub ready to start this journey, determined that if I tried hard enough, I could love enough for the both of us.

It worked for the honeymoon, but once we got home, reality set in and the fighting continued. I was about to start my career as a teacher in the fall, so I was not working that summer. In his mind, Don viewed me as lazy. If I was not working, I wasn't doing anything. I started making sure I had dinner and a drink ready for him when he got home for work. When that didn't work, I tried to watch what I said around him more and more.

I did not tell my family what was going on, but I did tell his. His mother, Helen, was sympathetic. She was my ear, my comfort. She had been going through similar stuff with the Don's father for most of their marriage, even leaving him at various times. She would commiserate with me.

His father was a different story. He would tell me that I needed to learn what not to do to set Don off. It was my fault that his son was so angry. I needed to learn how to communicate better with him and to work around his anger.

I began to turn things down—happy hours, baby showers, girl's nights—I worried that being away from him too much might set him off. After a particularly awful fight a year earlier, he had admitted that he was upset I was spending an entire week away from him, even though that week was to finish planning the wedding. I thought maybe spending more time together would help his anger.

I tried, especially in the first few months. Blair had come down to visit at the end of August, and we were all going to a Labor Day party hosted by friends of Don's parents. We got lost; neither of us could remember the directions clearly. But he blamed me and yelled at me in front of his friend, as well as calling me the usual names.

"You are such a dumb bitch. Why can't you do anything right?" he yelled.

"Dude, you've got to calm down. It's not her fault." I appreciated Blair trying to calm him down, and I gave him a sympathetic look.

I realized I needed to buck up. We were about to see family friends I had not seen since our wedding. So I sucked back the tears, fixed my makeup, and tried to forget my new husband had just berated me in front of one of our best friends.

When we showed up at the party, we both went our separate ways. Later, I was talking to a mutual friend who had just gotten engaged and was showing me her ring when Don walked by. I yelled to him to come over, and he snapped at me with such nastiness it caught the reaction of several people around me. When I felt fifty people turn and face me, I couldn't hold back the tears. I turned away to try and compose myself, and Blair grabbed my hand and led me to a secluded area of the massive property we were on.

"You are okay. Keep it together a little bit longer, Amanda," he kept repeating to me.

When we were finally completely alone, I collapsed. "Oh, Blair, I don't even know what I am doing. Why does he treat me like this?" I said. I began to sob uncontrollably.

"I don't know," he said. "It's not right. You don't deserve this."

I was still crying pretty hard when he grabbed me to turn and look at him. "Listen to me. Amanda, you don't deserve this. You are perfect." I cried harder but was comforted by the knowledge that someone thought I was worthy of love.

When Don rounded the corner and found us, he immediately softened. He apologized profusely for the way he was acting and told me again that if we needed to, we would go to therapy—he wanted the marriage to work.

As he hugged me, I looked over at Blair, who gave me a sympathetic look. This is what I wanted; I wanted my husband to acknowledge that the way he was acting was not appropriate. I wanted his apology and his sympathy, and I desperately wanted to make this marriage work.

My parents were both on their second marriages, as were both of my siblings. I was determined to be married for the rest of my life, like my grandparents, whose marriage lasted fifty years. I wanted to be one and done.

But while I wanted so desperately to make this marriage work, I knew it would only work if Don changed. If he truly took the time to work through his anger and stop the abuse. I believed him when he said that he did not want to act that way, and I believed that he knew he needed help but did not know how to get it.

But as I let him hug me and as I listened to him apologize, I came to a realization about what was happening in my new marriage. It was a realization I was not ready to yet vocalize or even let it be more than a fleeting thought: *this was abuse.* What he was doing to me was verbal abuse. What happened while we were engaged was physical abuse. I was being abused, and my new husband was my abuser. I was living in my very own made-for-TV movie. It was a lot to let sink in, and I was quieter that night than usual.

As was the cycle in our relationship, things got better and then they got worse. I started looking for patterns, wondering if maybe he had seasonal depression. I spoke to his mother and grandmother about my theory—and they agreed—so the three of us got him to start taking vitamin D supplements, desperately hoping that this would help. Therapy was not a reality yet.

The realization that I was scared of him came soon afterward. I was in my first year of teaching, and it was the night before I was to be observed by my principal. My principal was brand-new, like me, and no one really knew what to expect when it came to evaluations. I desperately wanted to make a good impression.

I had quite the class my first year, and I had spent a lot of time with the principal already because of discipline issues in my classroom. While I knew most of these incidents were not a reflection of my teaching, I still felt like it did not give the best impression and really wanted to knock his socks off with the lesson I had prepared.

Needless to say, I was a mess the night before. I tried to talk to Don about how nervous I was about the whole thing. He was sympathetic at first, but as the evening went on, his sympathy quickly waned. My mind was on my observation, not on making dinner or cleaning up, and I kept forgetting to do things because I was so distracted. His frustration grew by the minute. He reached his limit when I broke a glass while washing dishes.

When I looked up from the sink, I saw his eyes go black. I had seen this look once before, and I knew what was coming. He exploded, and I began crying and apologizing.

"You are so stupid. What the hell is wrong with you?"

"I'm sorry, I am so sorry. I will clean it up."

"You make a mess out of everything!"

He stormed upstairs, and I followed him, crying. Big mistake—as I was apologizing and trying again to explain how nervous I was, he shoved me against the wall. It hurt. A lot.

I told him through tears that he could not continue to physically hurt me. In response, he turned around and holding my arms at my side, began to headbutt me like before. He backed me into the hallway until I was teetering at the top of the stairs. I couldn't believe this was happening again—I was going to die or get seriously hurt. He was going to headbutt me till I fell down the stairs.

But he stopped. He stopped just as suddenly as he started. I was left standing in the hallway crying, rubbing my head and my arms. I looked down at my arms. He had been gripping me so hard that there were bruises.

I walked into the bedroom. He was sitting on the bed, his head in his hands. He did not tell me he was sorry this time; instead, he listed the reasons my behavior had set him off and told me that I needed to be better. I needed to learn how to control my anxiety and not let it affect him or our relationship.

I stood there, stunned. As I began apologizing, part of me realized how ridiculous it was. I was apologizing to the person who just physically and verbally abused me, but I just wanted it to stop. I wanted him to just stop treating me that way, and at that point, I would have done anything. I was scared that the next time he went after me physically, it would be my last. I just wanted it to stop.

He looked at me and told me that he forgave me. He then said the thing that I had desperately wanted to hear, from the moment I had said yes to his proposal.

"Maybe we should think about trying to have a baby."

Chapter 5:
And Baby Makes Three...Then Four!

*Havin my baby, what a lovely way of
sayin' how much you love me.*
—Paul Anka

HAVING A BABY CHANGES EVERYTHING, and I very naively thought it would change our relationship for the better. I thought having a baby would make him (and even me, a little bit) grow up. It would be a stressful but positive change for our relationship.

Honestly, trying for a child was the happiest we were during our entire marriage, and it wasn't just about all the sex we were having. It felt like we were finally a team, the team I always wanted to be.

I thought that we would try for a baby and then, poof! I would become pregnant right away, but it did not happen quite that way. It took six months to get pregnant with our son. In the grand scheme of things, six months is not a long time. For me, however, it felt like a lifetime.

When I took the pregnancy test, Don was at the gym. When I saw the word *pregnant,* I could not wait to tell him. I had thought about all the different ways I might tell him over the past six months, but in the end, I just blurted it out because I was so excited.

I cried as I told him. He looked shocked, like someone had just punched him in the gut, but I figured it was just shell shock. We called our families and friends, who were just as thrilled as we were—or at least as I was. Even his brother Colin—who shows no emotion, ever—told me over the phone how excited he was for us.

Don's shocked expression began to soften as the night went on, however, and we celebrated by having Chinese food and then lying in bed and talking about baby names.

He was quiet for several days afterward. I had already noticed that right as a big life event was happening (moving in together, getting married, a parent getting sick), his anger would increase—and Don did not deal with stress very well.

I was about to learn that me being pregnant was going to be very stressful.

I did not have a very easy pregnancy. I was sick, a lot, and was relying on him a lot as well. He was okay with it for the first week, but the thirty-six other weeks, not so much.

In the beginning of my pregnancy, the only things I could keep down was McDonald's chicken nuggets and lemonade. I was so worn out and sick all the time. It was a Saturday morning in August, and I was feeling particularly rough. I asked Don to go get me some food, hoping that would help, but he refused. He walked over to where I was, lying on the brown leather couch, and told me he was tired of being my slave and to go get it myself—we were on week nine at this point.

I looked at him in disbelief; I was carrying his child, and it was wreaking havoc on my body, both physically and mentally. And all I was asking him to do was stop playing video games and go up the road two miles to please get me something to eat.

I looked at him and walked out. I drove to a parking lot and just cried. I realized then how naïve I was and that I was now going to bring another life into this chaos that I called a marriage. I decided I was going to leave him.

I called his mother, Helen and told her. She very calmly asked me if I was seriously going to leave her son over chicken nuggets. No, I was not, I said. I was just upset he would not help me out while I was feeling so rotten.

What I was thinking was also no. I was not just leaving him over chicken nuggets, but I was leaving him because he was not willing to put my needs ahead of his. The bigger issue was, of course, that while

I had hoped the verbal abuse would stop now that I was pregnant, it had not. I was still being called names and being told I was worthless.

Eventually, I turned around, walked back into the house, and ignored my gut. Again.

The rest of my pregnancy was similar to the beginning. Me asking for help and trying to rely on my partner, Don being okay with it for a week or so, then getting annoyed I could not do as much as I used to. The verbal abuse ebbed and flowed throughout the pregnancy.

On March 3, 2014, we became parents to a beautiful baby boy, Ethan. His delivery was very eventful, as his heart rate kept fluctuating the entire time I was in labor. When I finally delivered, there were about thirty people in the room, ready to whisk him away. It turned out that he was squeezing the umbilical cord every time there was a contraction.

Don and I were beside ourselves with worry while I was in labor, and although Don was not there for me throughout my entire pregnancy, he showed up in a big way during delivery. He held my hand and got me ice chips when I needed them, and he told me how strong and brave I was. We both cried when we saw Ethan for the first time and heard his sweet cry.

I was in love instantly; I could have cared less about Don from that moment on, and he knew it. My priority shifted from trying to make the marriage work to making sure this little boy had the best life possible.

Having a baby is stressful, a kind of stress I never realized. To make matters worse, our son was jaundice, tongue-tied, colicky, and got every childhood disease known to man. The abuse had stopped for a few months as both of our attention was shifted toward this little boy, and I thought maybe this phase of his anger had stopped but again was wrong. He had just been saving and storing it until he exploded.

We had made our first trip up to Philadelphia as a family of three for Mother's Day. It was a stressful first trip with a two-month-old. We did not know what to bring, forgot half the stuff, and all of us barely slept while we were there.

On our way home, I asked him to stop at a rest stop, so I could change Ethan and feed him. The baby was not cooperating the whole car ride back and cried for what seemed like five hours. We pulled over, and I began to soothe Ethan. It was a beautiful May day, and I had rolled down the window, hoping that the fresh air would help calm Ethan down.

This was apparently the wrong move.

"You and that baby ruin everything," he said, just as our son finally stopped crying.

"I'm sorry, what?"

"You heard me. You are an awful mother. You can't multitask for shit. Look at our friends with multiple kids. They are so much better than you. You can barely even take care of him. You look like a disaster. Our house, our lives, all disasters."

He went on and on after that, but I blocked it out. I rocked Ethan to sleep as he continued to berate me. I did not hear a word he said after "awful mother." I was trying as hard as I could to take care of this little person and keep up with everything that fell under "my responsibility" at the house. I did feel like I was drowning, and he was confirming my worst fears: I was doing an awful job at the only job I have ever wanted. Being a mother.

I cried and cried. I cried the entire rest of the trip home. He snapped at me to stop crying, but I couldn't. How could I be failing this beautiful baby? What I could not see then was that this was another form of abuse. He was preying on me, knowing I was already worried I was failing.

The abuse kept coming, month by month, as our son grew. It was not unheard of when I would ask him for help, he would simply say no. "You wanted this, not me" was a common phrase of his.

One night, during bath time, I had asked him to come in and help. Ethan was about eight months old at the time and very wiggly. As he happily splashed around the tub, Don stormed in. I looked up at him as I was happily laughing with Ethan, and he said, "You and that baby have ruined my life!"

He stormed off just as quickly as he had come in. I looked at Ethan, who was still playing around, and tried to block out what my husband had just said to me.

When he had to stay home with the baby one day because Ethan had a fever, he was so infuriated that I called Helen and asked her to call him and come down. She assured me he would never hurt his child and made plans to come down. His mother did not stay long, however, as his father was rushed to the hospital with an undiagnosed ailment that would leave him in there for several days.

As before, any outside stress did not help. I knew it was going to be bad.

We had gone to the store and purchased several bottles of wine, but when I opened the trunk out smashed the bottles. He turned to me with that same black-eyed look.

"You are such a cunt! I cannot believe how stupid you are!" he yelled at the top of his voice.

I prayed that our neighbors did not hear him as he stood at the top of our stairs and yelled insult after insult at me as I struggled to bring the baby and the groceries in, as well as clean up the mess.

He did not help, just kept yelling and calling me awful names over and over again. I looked him in the eye and saw the anger. Then, I looked at my beautiful baby boy and decided I was done. He would not get to talk to me like this in front of our child anymore—I was going to do what I should have done months, years ago.

I walked past him, went upstairs, and started packing a bag for myself and for the baby.

"Where the hell are you going? You are not taking my son!" He started coming after me. I grabbed Ethan, and he chased me around the house. I should have called 911, but I called his mother instead. She tried to talk to him, but he just kept saying that I was a cunt.

I finally looked at him, grabbed the bags I packed and walked past him. I put the baby in the car and pulled out of the driveway. I did not know what to do or where to go. I called our mutual friends, Cheryl and Rick, who were the only real friends I had in Virginia at the time. Cheryl stayed on the phone with me while I did the ten-minute drive to their house.

When I showed up, Rick passed me in the driveway. He said he was going to go talk to Don and find out what was going on. He told me to stay put at their house and that I was safe. I cried and cried, sitting on their couch. I watched my son play on the floor with Cheryl's son, who is just a week older than him. I felt such guilt for messing up this beautiful child's life by bringing him into this world.

Rick eventually came back and told me that Don was ready to talk. He assured me I was safe and that I should try and talk to him.

I drove back. Why go back? I wanted to believe that this would get better. I wanted to believe that this was the last fight like this and that Ethan would be able to grow up in a two-parent household. But I was terrified at what I would find. Would he still be angry? Would he hurt me? Or would he start just apologizing like he had in the past?

It was anger that I was met with. He told me he had already called our parents and told them that we were getting a divorce. I was shocked and called my parents crying.

My mom said she did not believe him and was going to call me later to see what was going on. My dad got on the phone with Don and told him that this was not the right move. My dad asked me point-blank if Don had yelled at me or laid a hand on me. I lied and said no. I did not want my parents to know that I was staying in an abusive marriage. I was ashamed of what this had turned into. I still am.

I called my friends and my sister. I felt like it was time to stop hiding what Don had become. I did not tell them everything, but I did tell them about this fight. They were all minutes away from calling the police, but I talked them down. I told them I wanted to stay.

A few hours later, Don asked me to come downstairs. He apologized and told me he could not believe the way he acted. I looked him straight in the eye and told him that I would not be treated like this anymore. I was not going to take this, and I was not going to have our son be brought up in a house with this abuse. He understood, and he said he would do whatever he had to do to keep our family together.

I believed him, but I was hurt. I slept in the guest room, and the next day, I started researching divorce attorneys.

Two days later, I found out I was pregnant with our daughter.

I had wanted to have more than one child, but I had also realized that I had no business bringing another baby into the little family that I had created. As I stared down at the pregnancy test, the words *pregnant* burned into my eye sockets. How in the hell did this happen?

Don't get me wrong, I remember how it happened. I thought we were being somewhat careful, but apparently, we were not. Now, I had to tell Don.

He was sitting on the couch with Ethan, who had just fallen asleep in his arms. I looked at him with tears in my eyes.

"What's wrong? Are you okay? Did something happen?" he asked.

"I'm pregnant." I was barely able to get the words out before crying.

He looked at me and grabbed my hand. "Everything is going to be okay. We are going to be okay, I promise," he said.

I believed him. I was scared. I was scared for the child we already had and for the one that I was now pregnant with.

I believed him because I felt like I had to. I was barely holding on looking after one baby, now I was going to have two. There was no way I was going to be able to handle both babies on my own. I needed him. I needed his financial support, and I was hoping I could count on his emotional support as well this time around.

If I thought my first pregnancy was rough, it was nothing compared to what I experienced the second time around. In addition to being nauseous all the time, I was in a tremendous amount of pain—my body had not healed from the first time. Don had no choice but to step up and for all his faults he did.

Most of the caregiving for our now one-year-old son was still on me. He was an awful sleeper and was still waking up several times in the middle of the night. Being heavily pregnant while trying to put another baby in a crib was no easy task. One night, trying to put him back in his crib, I screamed out in pain.

Don came running into the room to help me and soothe Ethan, whom I had scared. He told me not to worry and that he would help. The next day, he put a stack of telephone books by our son's crib so that I could step on them to put our son back in his crib.

I was put on modified bed rest for the last month of my pregnancy. My mother and his took turns coming down to help, and Don was great for the first week, but then, it went downhill.

We began fighting again. Just about everyday stuff. He started telling me how me being on bedrest affected him negatively, and I found myself crying and apologizing a lot, not always knowing what was pissing him off. I just wanted him to stop.

On August 23, 2015, we had a beautiful little girl, Tessa Ann. Her birth was much more relaxed than Ethan's had been, and I fell in love all over again.

The minute she was placed in my arms, I knew she was going to a force to be reckoned with. Newborns are supposed to just lay there—not Tessa. Her mouth kept moving like she was trying to talk to me, and none of her limbs would stay still. She was going to be a handful, I immediately started worrying about how this would affect Don.

Don was great again in the delivery room, doing and saying all the right things, but it took exactly two hours after I gave birth for us to have an explosive fight, right there in my hospital room.

Chapter 6:
Enough

Nobody put's baby in in the corner.
—Patrick Swayze, *Dirty Dancing*

"YOU ARE SO STUPID! You are worthless! How could you let this happen? I'm going to divorce you, and no judge will ever let you see the kids because of how financially irresponsible you are! You ruin everything!"

I know exactly where I was standing when I realized I finally had had enough, and I was done.

Our children were five and three, and I was washing dishes in our brand-new house when he started screaming at me—spitting on me—just inches from my face.

He was upset my credit score had gotten dinged from an Amazon bill that I had never received. I was finally able to get away from him, which took some maneuvering. It was almost as if we were doing some weird dance: as I would go left to walk around him, he would follow. He eventually gave up, muttered something under his breath, and stormed into the basement.

I will never forget what I saw as I rounded the corner to go check on the children. It will be imprinted in my brain for the rest of my life. The kids were huddled together, holding hands, and Ethan was telling Tessa it was okay, everything was going to be okay. Tessa had tears streaming down her face. That is when I knew I had to get out.

There was a change that happened in the two of us when our second child was born. I don't know if it was because she was a girl or that I simply did not have time to deal with his abuse anymore. I stopped caring what he thought, and he stopped caring if he hurt me. Time after time, he would call me names and yell at me in front of our two small children. My only hope was that they were too small to realize what he was saying or what was going on. Words like *cunt*, *bitch*, or just calling me *woman* were now normalized in our house, as were statements about how stupid or worthless I was.

"What if someone talked to our daughter the way you talked to me? Would you be okay with that?" I would ask him.

"I would never be okay if she acted the way you act." This was his rebuttal, time after time.

I knew it was him and not me, but I was still determined to do everything I could to try and hold this family together. I wanted so desperately for my children to grow up in a two-person household. Constantly walking on eggshells was worth it to me if it meant my kids could wake up every morning with both their mom and their dad.

But I slowly began to realize that I was doing more damage to my children by staying in an abusive relationship than I would by leaving. Both children began to feel the brutality of his anger. He began to call them names and get angry with them over even the smallest of things. I began to be fearful of any time he was alone with the children. I rearranged my schedule at work so I could leave a little early and be the one to pick the children up from school. I had come home one to many times to everyone in tears and Don barely able to speak because he was so angry at them. Please bear in mind that he had them for a total of forty minutes before I would walk through the door.

He had screamed at Tessa one night because she would have a hard time falling asleep. We split the children up at bedtime, and I usually took Ethan, who had a hard time sleeping, historically, and Don took Tessa. But our little girl began to have a hard time falling asleep at night and this frustrated Don to no end. He wanted our two toddlers to act like mini adults instead.

On this particular night, she was having an unusually hard time falling asleep. I had just finished putting our son to bed, and I was walking from the bedroom when I heard yelling. As I moved closer, I froze.

"Go the fuck to sleep!" he bellowed to our two-year-old daughter.

I instantly went into protective mode. "You can't talk to her like that!"

"Fuck you! She ruins everything!" Don stormed past me.

I looked in at Tessa. She was sobbing. I grabbed her and held her. I told her she was safe and that I would always protect her. I told her she was loved and that Daddy did not mean what he said. I soothed her and held her till she was able to peacefully go to sleep.

When I came out of her room, I had no idea where Don was, and frankly, I did not care. I could not believe he went after our child like that.

I took over putting her to bed, but it did not solve her sleeping issues. My son began to act out at school. While I would tell Don I was unsure why this was happening, I knew. I knew that their behavior was in direct correlation as to what was happening in their home. The abuse that they witnessed, and that was beginning to be directed toward them, was having an effect.

I did not know what to do. The clear answer is to just leave, for our own safety. But I was worried. How could I protect them from a nasty divorce? How could I make sure that his abuse did not then turn its focus on them if I was not around? Who would protect them from his anger?

That moment in the kitchen, with him inches from my face, I knew something had to change. I needed to protect my children, but I also knew I could not stay in this house, this marriage, or this family without it having dire consequences for both my children and for myself.

But how did I go about doing this in the safest way possible? There was a real concern that he would hurt me or the children if I tried to leave.

I was also feeling pretty down on myself. I did not want to be alone, and I definitely did not want to be a single mom. I was not even sure what I could afford on a teacher salary. I wondered who would ever want me now, an abused single mother with two small children.

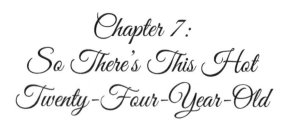

Chapter 7:
So There's This Hot
Twenty-Four-Year-Old

Oh hell, he'd look hot in a chicken suit.
                                    —Cyn Balog

LET ME BE PERFECTLY CLEAR: I did not cheat. At least, not phys-ically. However, what I experienced during the last month of my marriage was definitely a spark I had never had before with someone...ever.

During that summer, I worked at one of the premiere day camps in Northern Virginia. The director happened to be Don's best friend, so needless to say, my sweet summer gig with seventy-five percent off tuition for my kids ended when my marriage did.

I have worked there on and off since I was pregnant with my son. The staff consists mainly of twenty-somethings. It was fun to work there, and it quickly became my happy place, the summer I realized I needed out of my abusive marriage. I could laugh and feel safe with a group of people who genuinely appreciated me and wanted to be around me.

Especially my friend, Nate. Or as I referred to him, the hot twenty-four-year-old.

Nate and I had met the previous summer. Ever meet someone and forget your own name? Me neither, until I met Nate.

One day, I had to hunt him down on the sprawling campus of the day camp. I can't remember why, but the problem was I had no idea who he was and what he looked like. I had been down to where he worked and around where he would take his break, but no one knew where he was.

I had given up and was headed back to my office when I spotted him. He was gorgeous. I stopped dead in my tracks. He was tall, dark, and handsome, and his muscles bulged out of his t-shirt. Normally, I would mock someone for this, but on him, it looked hot.

I could not tell you what I said, or what he said for that matter. All I know is that for the first time in my life, I was standing in front of a man, and I did not want him to stop talking. I can still hear his laugh in my head.

He stopped by my office from time to time after that. I caught him staring at me and had to stop myself from staring too long at him. I reminded myself that I was married, even if I was unhappy.

It was a different story the summer I realized my marriage was over. Nate and I began to work closely together on an administrative issue, and I found myself making excuses to talk to him. He would do the same. If we were not talking in person, we could be found texting each other throughout the day.

He was slated to leave the day camp while I was on my family vacation, and I did not want to leave, not because I did not want to go to the beach but because I was pretty sure this hot twenty-four-year-old was flirting with me and I liked it. I did not want it to end. It made me feel special, a feeling I had not had in quite some time.

I said goodbye to him, awkwardly. It was a half-hug, half-hand-shake, mixed with a high five. Not my best moment. As I trudged down the stairs from my office, I figured that was that—until he reached out the following Sunday.

I may have been out of the game for a while, but I knew he must be looking for an excuse to talk to me. He asked me to check on a few staff members that he was worried about, and we talked throughout day.

One day, while helping with the daily camper pick up—depending on the week, it can be a long process, with upwards of five hundred campers—I looked up from my clipboard, and I saw him. As he strutted down the driveway and headed right for me, it was like an '80s movie. There was a big part of me that wanted to run into his arms and lay a kiss on him but that didn't seem like the most appropriate course of action, so I just stood there, awkwardly. I made a joke about wanting to hit him for leaving me alone to deal with a mess.

When we walked into my office, the energy between us was palpable. By the look in his eyes, I knew I wasn't the only one who felt that way, and when he grabbed my hand and held on a half-second too long, I was sure.

We began a flirty text chain over the next few weeks. It took me away from the stress of my real life, which was anything but wonderful. In addition to my workload, I was being told, on a daily basis at this point, how truly stupid, lazy, and worthless I was—or just got the silent treatment.

Nate became the person I turned to when I was stressed and the person I most looked forward to speaking to every day. There was not a day that went by that one of us did not reach out to the other.

One night, he asked me how I met Don. "Figured I should learn as much as I can about my competition," he wrote.

Holy shit, this hot twenty-four-year-old was into me. Me, a thirty-six-year-old married woman with two small children. Me, who was told constantly that I was nothing. He was into me.

I told him that I believed my husband was not my biggest fan.

"I doubt that," he texted back. "Who would hate you?"

Yup, I liked the way he made me feel. He told me he would come to the camp that Wednesday afternoon to tie up some loose ends with counselors before the summer ended.

"Well, that's my excuse for coming. I'm really coming to see you," he wrote.

I had mixed feelings; his flirting made me feel good. It made me realize that someone, other than Don, could want me. That the awful things I was being told about myself by Don were not true. It was empowering, but it also began to feel very wrong. While I knew I wanted out of my marriage, I was still married, and this was about as far as I was willing to go.

I was nervous to see him. When he arrived, my heart skipped a beat. He helped me handle some issues, and then, we sat and talked for about two hours. It was nice to have someone else want to hear my voice and opinions on things.

He walked me down to pick up my two children, whom he knew well at this point. While we walked, I swallowed the knot that had been building up in my throat and asked, "Why do you flirt with me so much? I can't tell if this is just BS or if you seriously have feelings for me."

Well, that stopped him dead in his tracks. "Well, how serious are you?"

"No," I said, "I'm not playing that game. I asked you first."

He paused, "About 80/20."

"Okay." I had no idea what the hell that meant, but I didn't know what I actually wanted that answer to be.

"Why?" he asked.

"I was just wondering."

"Liar. Why'd you ask?"

"Honestly..." We were interrupted by my two children running at us. They were excited to see Nate, and he carried my daughter to the car. This was a pivotal moment for me: another man carried my daughter to the car. It was a sign.

He placed her in her car seat, and we said another awkward goodbye.

He texted me later that night and said, "Honestly, I am one hundred percent serious...is that bad?"

I'm not here to say that we went on to have a hot steamy love affair. Or that he rescued me from an abusive marriage and showed me that I could be loved the way I deserved to be loved. None of that happened. That part of our relationship fizzled as quickly as it started, and to this day, he is a very dear friend of mine. But just that, a friend.

What he showed me that summer was that all the lies I had been told for the better part of ten years were simply that—lies. Knowing someone young, hot, and sexy, who wanted me, did more for me than I will ever be able to accurately express. It gave me strength, and without that strength, I do not know if I could have gotten through what happened next.

Chapter 8:
August 3, 2019

If you ever find yourself in the wrong story, leave.
—Mo Willems

SOMETHING WAS WRONG. I COULD not put my finger on it—was it Don? Maybe. Was it just something in the universe? Possibly. But when I woke up on the morning of August 3, 2019, I knew something was definitely wrong.

We were getting ready to leave for a week-long family cruise to the Caribbean the next day. My father was taking the entire family, and everyone was excited. Don seemed a little anxious, but I ignored it and focused on getting the kids ready.

He took Ethan to get a haircut, and I took Tessa to get a manicure and pedicure. My little girl loves a good manicure and pedicure—I will never forget the look on her face when she was getting her first manicure. It was as if she was saying in her head, "Yes, these are my people!"

Don and I met back at home for lunch. He was already in a prickly mood, and I had sent Tessa to her room as soon as we walked back into the house. While she loves her manicures and pedicures, she wants to leave as soon as she is done, which had resulted in an epic meltdown.

As we began eating lunch, Don started complaining about how poorly our neighbor's child was acting the previous night. At the same time, Tessa's tantrum was continuing upstairs.

"How can you complain about someone else's child when our own is doing that upstairs?" I asked.

"You are impossible! I can't even talk to you anymore. You are just so abrasive all the time!" He stormed off.

I sat there and wondered to myself what exactly had happened. He was complaining about one child's behavior while the one we made was currently performing a one-woman reenactment of *The Exorcist*.

When he eventually came back up, I tried to talk to him, but he gave me the silent treatment. I gave him some space until a few hours later, when the kids were playing outside with their friends.

"Will you please talk to me? We are supposed to be going on a family trip with my whole family tomorrow. I don't want to fight today," I pleaded.

He turned to me, looked me in the eye, and said, "I will wait until the kids are 18, but I want a divorce the minute that happens." And then he walked away.

I stood there thinking, *Excuse me, what? You want a divorce? No, that's my line!*

I was worried. We were about to go on a cruise with my whole family, and my husband just announced that in fifteen years we were going to divorce. I did not know which end was up.

I called my sister, Tara, and the minute I heard her voice, I began to sob. I unloaded on her—not about the abuse but about the fighting and the name-calling. I told her that I did not know what to do.

"Amanda, do you want a divorce?" she asked.

"I don't know."

"And I don't know is an answer," Tara said. She was right. I was more concerned about what my parents were going to say. Tara asked to speak to Don so she could try and reason with him.

When I told him my sister was on the phone and she wanted to talk to him, he said he wanted nothing to do with my family, loud enough for her to hear.

"Here is what we are going to do," Tara said. "You are going to get those kids and get on the cruise tomorrow without him. We are going to spend all week together as a family and get a plan together to get you out of this marriage."

I knew this would be her response. I knew this would be everyone's response once I told them what was really going on. I had not been ready to hear it, but I was ready now.

When I got off the phone, he exploded. He was furious that I would call my sister and tell her what was going on. He told me that under no circumstances was he going on that cruise tomorrow, and he certainly was not going to attend the retirement party that we were supposed to go to that evening.

As I began getting ready for the party, he began hurling insults at me again, "You are the worst mother. You are constantly leaving the kids. I hope you got a babysitter because I am going out. I am tired of you always leaving me to take care of the kids."

These were lies. I walked over to my neighbors' house and asked if they would mind watching the kids while I went out for two hours, so I could stop by this party. Jackie and I became good friends the moment we met after moving to the neighborhood, and she and her husband, Jackson, quickly became like family to us. We shared many dinners and vacations together.

I told Jackie briefly what was going on and she said to send the kids over and that she and her husband would reach out to Don.

Tessa, having calmed down earlier, was already at Jackie's house, playing with her kids. I went inside to talk to Ethan. I told him that I was going out just for a little bit, but I would be home for bedtime. I told him he had to go to Jackie and Jackson's for dinner and I would pick him up there.

"Wait, where's Daddy going?" he asked as he turned to Don, who was standing behind us.

"I'm going to the strip club. I'm tired of having kids dumped on me."

My five-year-old son looked at me, confused, but I told him not to worry and that he was going to have McDonald's for dinner with his friends. He skipped over to our neighbor's house happily, and I got into my car.

On the way to the retirement party, I called my friends to tell them what was going on. There was no sense in hiding what my marriage had become. I was going to follow my sister's advice and figure out how to safely get away from him.

I went to the retirement party, and I will never for one-minute regret that I did. It was a bright spot in an awful day. I got to go and be with people that I consider family, my coworkers. I laughed until my sides hurt and felt genuinely loved, which I desperately needed.

As I was at the party, Jackie texted me to tell me she talked to Don and that he loves me and will be going on the cruise the next day. I ignored it; this was no longer his decision. In fact, nothing in my life was his decision anymore.

I drove home and picked my kids up. Don had apparently already walked back to our house. When the three of us walked in, he was sitting on the couch. I walked the kids upstairs and got them in the shower.

We have a huge shower, perfect for washing toddlers. Don came up to get our son ready for bed, but our son told him that he wasn't ready and turned to me and asked if he could have a few more minutes to play. I said yes, and Don stormed off.

I got the kids out and dried them. I told our son to tell his dad to get him ready for bed. He walked off but came back a minute later, crying hysterically.

"What happened? What's wrong?" I asked him.

"Daddy just yelled at me. He said, 'Go to bed yourself you little shit.'"

It was unbelievable, but at the same time, there was not a bone in my body that did not believe that Don said exactly that.

I calmed both of the kids down. I got them ready for bed, read two stories, and made sure they were both calm and okay before I went downstairs to address Don. It is one thing to come after me, but I was done allowing him to go after our children.

"What the hell?" I said. He ignored me.

"You can't talk to him like that. He's just a child." He still ignored me.

"Get your ass up and go make up with your son!"

That got his attention. He told me to go fuck myself and then walked away. I followed him up the stairs, telling him how incredibly unacceptable to speak to a child like that. I was pushing him to talk to me; I knew that deep down he knew I was right on this matter. He was beginning to speak to our children the way his father spoke to him as a child, and he hated that.

He turned to me and threw the glass of water he was holding all over me. I was soaked.

The yelling started then. I don't remember what either of us said at first. I was determined to not let him get away with this again. This was going to be the last time he ever pushed me around. I told him that if he did not stop, I was going to call the police.

"Call the police? Go ahead. You will be dead before they get here. I will have your body chopped up before they even ring the doorbell," he said this while staring at me nose to nose.

I ran down the stairs, my cell phone in hand, when I realized I had a fatal flaw in my plan. He was at the top of the stairs—he was between me and the children. I had to get the kids.

"What are you going to do, Amanda? Are you going to call the cops?" he asked in a mocking tone.

When I didn't respond, he continued. "You know what, fuck this. I am going to burn this house down. I'm getting the gas can and burning this to the ground. You won't even have time to get the kids out."

I froze as he passed by me on the stairs and headed out to the garage. The minute he was out of sight, I ran upstairs into the kids' rooms. I told them to grab their lovies and that we had to leave right then.

They followed me out of the house and over to Jackie and Jackson's house. As I turned back, I saw Don rounding the corner with the gas can in one hand and a lighter in the other. I had gotten the kids and myself out in time.

I was terrified. I looked down at my two children. I have since tried everything I can think of to forget the look on both of their faces, but I am sure I never will. It was something more than fear that they were experiencing.

I called 911 as we banged on my Jackie's door, screaming into the phone for the police to come.

As Jackson opened the door, Don walked out of our house. I was terrified that he was going to shoot us all dead right then and there, but instead, he got into his car and peeled out of the driveway. As he drove off, he yelled, "Nice knowing you, bitch."

Part 2

Chapter 9:
The Aftermath

It's ok to fall apart sometimes. Tacos
fall apart; we still love them.
—Unknown

MY HUSBAND HAD JUST THREATENED to kill me and my children; that was my new reality. After Don had driven off, Jackson, who also happens to be a police officer, walked me back to my house, where I was greeted by three other police officers.

After talking to them, they told me that based on the information I had just given them, pressing charges was out of my hands. Don would be arrested and was going to spend some time in jail. I was going to be granted an emergency protective order that would be good for three days. If I wanted it extended, I would have to appear that Monday at court to get a two-week extension.

I sat on my stairs, numb. Stairs that I ran down earlier, fearing for my life and the lives of my children. I texted my sister and my friends to tell them what was currently going on in my house. I figured while I was numb, I should just get it over with telling as many people at once as I could stomach.

The worst was telling my parents. After an hour, the police left to meet Don, who was going to turn himself in. Instantly, my parents and I began crying. They would be making the trip down from Philadelphia first thing in the morning. I didn't argue.

The kids came back. I think they were numb as well. Tessa asked me if Daddy was really going to shoot me, and Ethan wanted to make sure we had working smoke detectors. I set them both up in my bedroom, in my bed. I turned the TV on for them to one of their favorite shows, told them I loved them, and walked back downstairs to wait for the police officer who would be delivering my protective order. I should have done more for the kids in that moment, but I could barely function. I poured myself a glass of bourbon and waited on my front steps.

The officer came back with my protective order and instructed me that I should go to get the extension on Monday. He strongly advised me not to go on the cruise. He also informed me that since children were involved and that he was a mandated reporter, he had to call Child Protective Services. I knew CPS well. As a teacher, I had experienced the unpleasantness of having to call them from time to time. I never thought there would be a call placed for my own children.

Jackson came back and announced he was going to sleep on my couch; I appreciated it. I walked upstairs and stared at my two beautiful children. I felt such a deep sense of guilt and pain—I could not believe I allowed it to get this bad. I vowed to make sure that I would never again put myself, or them, in a situation where our safety, both physical and mental, was compromised.

The next morning, I woke early. That is a lie: I did not sleep. I think I may have drifted off briefly, but I was quickly jolted awake, remembering that this was not all a dream. I felt as if I had the worst hangover headache of my life.

I immediately called Blair and his new wife, Kristin. I knew I was going to wake them up, but I also knew they would not mind. I explained what happened, and he said he was on his way. He would do whatever I needed done, which was change locks and change passwords.

I called the day camp director, Don's best friend, and explained what had happened. I did not care at that moment whose side he and his wife would eventually take. What was more important to me was that the kids could come to camp the next day to keep some normalcy in their lives. He said of course and that whatever I needed, he was here for me.

When the kids woke up and came downstairs, I held them tightly. I told them I was so sorry they were so scared last night, but I would always protect them. I then had to break the news that we could no longer go on the trip they were so looking forward to. They were upset, but the misery subsided when I told them they could have candy for breakfast and stay in their pajamas all day.

Blair, Kristin, and my parents arrived. I met them all in the driveway. Within seconds of seeing me, everyone was crying. How could this happen? How could they not know that this was happening?

Blair went right to work, looking at what he needed to get to change the locks, and Kristin went to the kids. To say that the kids love Kristin—or Aunt KiKi, as they call her—is a vast understatement, and her presence was a comforting one, for them and for me.

My parents and I stayed in the driveway to talk. I did not realize how badly I needed them until I saw their faces and felt their embrace.

"Are you okay?"

"Are you physically hurt?"

"Did he hurt the kids?"

"I'm going to kill him, and if I don't, your brother will." My father, ladies and gentlemen.

I assured them that physically I was okay, mentally, I did not know what was going on. I knew I had to go to the courthouse tomorrow to get an extension of the protective order. I also knew I needed a lawyer, possibly two. My mother was on it and was going to call some friends in the area for recommendations. They also said they were staying indefinitely.

We were interrupted by my phone ringing. It was Helen.

I hesitated to pick it up; I had just sent her son to jail. I knew, years prior, when there was abuse, she had said she would call the police if ever there was a next time. I was also distinctly aware that this was her son, and she most certainly would take his side in any matter.

She was cool on the phone, and I gave her short one-word answers.

"Well, you certainly seem to be handling this well," Helen said in possibly the most sarcastic tone I had ever heard from her.

I lost it. How dare she? Her son had just threatened to kill me and our children. I told her how not okay I was and that it was entirely her son's fault. She then proceeded to tell me how sorry he was and that he loved me. I was silent.

"Well, Amanda. I don't know what else there is to say."

Nothing. There was nothing left to say. I simply hung up.

Blair called me downstairs after I had hung up with Helen. "Amanda, you know your safe was open."

Yes, I knew we had a black fireproof safe where we stored important documents. I assumed one of us had been in it to collect the passports and had simply forgotten to close it.

"Yeah, I think I forgot to close it," I yelled down.

"Oh, so you know these stacks of red envelopes with money are here."

What? I ran downstairs to see what he was talking about. Sure enough, the safe was open, and there was a stack of money. I counted it: $4,800. I counted it again. Still $4,800.

"Why would he keep this much money and not tell me it even existed?" I asked Blair.

"No idea, but I guess it's yours now."

I was in disbelief. I paid for everything with the kids and struggled to do so. He made significantly more money than I did, but I was responsible for all the grocery shopping, most of the utilities, daycare, sports, and anything else the kids might need. Most of the time, I had some sort of credit card debt and here he was, sitting on almost $5,000 in our basement. I knew exactly what I was going to do with it.

Chapter 10:
These are Going to be the Worst Days of My Life

Know when to give up and have a margarita.
—Unknown, or every-
one on Cinco de Mayo

"I'M SORRY, YOU'RE CALLING FROM where?"

"This is Diane from Child Protective Services. I received a call about an incident that happened at your home involving the children on August 3, 2019. I need to come out and speak to you. Are you available this evening?"

I managed to stammer out a yes and hung up. I collapsed and Hannah, my officemate for the summer, grabbed me and hugged me.

It had been three days since what I considered the worst day of my life. I was barely hanging on. My parents had stayed, and without their help, I don't know how I would have managed it in those early days without them. They made dinner, helped with getting the kids dressed and ready, and maintaining a somewhat normal schedule.

The Monday following "the incident," I found myself at court filing the paperwork to extend my protective order. I had to describe what happened the night of August 3 over and over again. Each time I thought it would get easier, but it did not.

I was told I needed to appear before a judge to explain why I wanted a protective order. The caseworker who was assigned to me that day prepped me. He told me I had to tell the judge I was scared;

that was the only way I was going to get one. This was not a lie—I was scared.

I had heard from mutual friends that he was a mess, crying all the time and that he just wanted to get back to me and the kids. I knew this was a phase; eventually, the anger would set in. That is what I was worried about.

The caseworker also told me that as a mandated reporter he was going to have to call CPS as well. It didn't get any easier hearing that a second time.

I had never been in a courtroom before in my life, nor had I ever been so nervous. It was incredibly intimidating sitting in a courtroom in front of a judge. I stated my name and began to tell my story. Eventually, the judge stopped me, and I started crying.

"Ms. Lee, I've heard enough. I am granting your two-week extension for a protective order. The hearing date will be two weeks from this date."

The first part of the story had been enough for the judge, and I was given the protective order. She did not even need to hear the details of the gas can or me pulling my children out of bed. I should have been happy, but I felt more scared and alone than ever.

I knew I needed to get a lawyer. I pulled the list that my mom had gotten from her friend out of my pocket and called the first name I saw. I called and pleaded with the assistant who answered to have her boss call me back the minute she had a chance.

The worst part of this whole process was having to tell the story over and over again. The reactions of people were awful—most were in disbelief, a few cried. Having to walk a copy of the protective order into the kid's school was especially bad, as was telling their teachers to please give them some grace and extra hugs as we navigated our new normal.

When you have a protective order, you end up having to tell everyone and making copy after copy of it. I had to have a meeting with my principal and assistant principal to let them know what had happened and that I would be out quite a bit for court appearances (for the record, my entire school community was nothing short of amazing during all of this). I made copies and told every babysitter that came into my house. I made sure there was a copy of the protective order on me at all times, as well as in the house, the car, and my classroom.

When I got home after my first court appearance, there were two letters waiting for me. The first was a court summons—there was to be a criminal hearing for what Don had done. The second was a letter from an attorney Don had hired, requesting to see the kids and requesting items he needed from the house.

He wanted to see the kids? Had he lost his mind? There was no way I was going to allow this man anywhere near my children. It was now more urgent than ever that I find attorneys.

The attorney called me back, and we set up an appointment to meet with her and her colleague. I was going to need two lawyers: one criminal to help navigate the hearing and all the protective order stuff, and the second for the divorce.

As I contemplated how this was actually my life, the doorbell rang. It was Diane, from CPS. I asked to speak to her outside on the front porch. I was doing my best to shield the kids from any talk about what was going on. I knew they did not need to hear the details of that night or to hear negative things about their father.

I went through the events, again, with her. She asked to come into the house and see where everything happened and asked to see the children's rooms. She came in and introduced herself to both children. She looked around the kitchen and asked to see inside the refrigerator and the pantry.

We then went out back to speak further. I was nervous; I told her how surreal this was for me. As an educator, I was the one who normally had to call CPS. I never imagined CPS would be called on me.

She corrected me, "I was not called because of something you did. I was called because of what he did."

While that was comforting, it was still nerve-racking. I told her how I was going to try and find a therapist for the children to talk to. She said that was an excellent idea and told me that I needed to find someone too. I knew this, but right now, my priority was making sure the kids were okay. I would deal with my feelings later.

"Ms. Lee, you are doing everything right. The problem with domestic violence victims is that nine times out of ten, the victim goes back with the abuser. I am going to start an investigation into possible child abuse and or neglect against your husband. It is not against you at the moment. However, if you let him back in the house, you and I will be having a very different conversation."

I knew the minute the police showed up that night that we were going to get a divorce, so the idea of letting him back into the house never even crossed my mind. There was no turning back. I know there are people who go through something like this and are able to go to counseling and then work things out. This was not us.

This was my ticket out, but I was fearful. There was a great fear of the unknown; I didn't know if I could make it as a single mother. I had been told for years that I was stupid and that I was not financially responsible. How could I provide for myself and two children?

But I felt like my hand was forced that night. I was not given a chance to weigh the pros and cons. I was not given the chance to think about what my life was going to be like as a single mother. The fear of the unknown was not given a chance that night and the denial of the abuse by my husband went out the window. I had seconds to think, seconds to act.

My door had been forced open, and I was going to walk through it.

Chapter 11:
You Say Therapist, I Hear Psychic

It's like I have ESPN or something.
—Amanda Seyfried, *Mean Girls*

"I SAW A PSYCHIC."

"I'm sorry, you did what?" I had to look at the phone to make sure I had called the right person. I was on the phone with Sue, my fiery redheaded friend since childhood. I had just met with my two new best friends, my lawyers, so I was overwhelmed and felt like I was drowning. When we got on the phone, Sue said she had something to tell me.

"Mand, it was good. She was telling me things about my ex, the kids, and my future. And she gave really good advice."

"Seriously?" I believe in all this stuff but Sue? No way. I once brought tarot cards over to her house when we were kids, and she laughed me out of her room. If she was believing this woman, I knew I needed to talk to her.

"Okay, I'm in. What's her name and how do I see her?" I asked.

"I have no idea. I think she is based in the South. She was up in Philly for an event. I think she's really hard to get an appointment with too. She has celebrity clients. Her name is Bonni McCliss."

I went home, googled her, and made an appointment. Sue was right, I could not get a phone appointment right away. I did not think twice about spending $80 on the call. I knew this was right. She could help me see where my life might be heading, and I was starting to have major anxiety about my future.

I had been trying so hard to keep my marriage and family together. When I realized, well before August 3, this could not continue, I never allowed myself to think of the future. I knew if I began to think about what my life was going to look like in the future, I would never leave him.

I thought maybe talking to someone who could see what might be in store for me would be comforting, even if some of it never came true. While I waited for my first appointment with Bonni, I had my first court appearance with Don. I knew this was going to be hard but not how hard.

I arrived an hour before the hearing with my parents. I tried to go by myself but they insisted. In the end, I was relieved I was not alone.

My attorney had told me what to expect. He said that his attorney would ask for a continuation of the hearing until after the criminal proceedings had taken place. We would only be in the courtroom for five minutes. What he had not prepped me for was seeing Don for the first time since that night.

As we walked up to the courthouse, I froze. There he was. He froze too. It was not nerves anymore. What I felt was fear, paralyzing fear. I spun around and walked even faster. I didn't want to say anything to my parents, honestly, because I was worried my dad would actually kill him right there and then in front of the courthouse.

I went through security and saw his grandmother. I had never even thought of who he would have with him, and it was a little jarring to see her standing there. She had never liked me, and I was prepared to ignore her. When I walked through the metal detector, however, she enveloped me in a hug. I was not ready for that. I don't remember what she said to me, but all I kept thinking was that she was only being nice because she had yet to realize that I was going to divorce him.

My attorney was correct, the whole thing took about five minutes, but it felt like five hours. I tried my best to hold in my tears, but I couldn't; they just started flowing. As I cried, and the sheriff handed me tissues, I heard sobbing from the other side of the courtroom. I thought it was my mom or his grandmother at first, but it was him.

I was trying my best to assume that the display was sincere when my attorney turned to me and said, "No way those are real tears. He better not try this during the criminal proceedings. They will throw him into jail for bad acting."

It made me laugh. I walked out of the courtroom and tried to compose myself. I switched on my phone and had two voicemails. The first from Bonni, confirming our appointment coming up, and the second from Ethan's school. He had thrown up and I had to rush over to get him.

I listened to the voicemails with tears still streaming down my cheek. There was no one else to call to see if they could get him. I needed to leave straight from the courtroom to go pick him up. I realized then that this was now my life as a single mother.

The next day as I was driving my children to their very first therapy appointment, my phone rang. It was a Nashville number.

"Hi, Amanda it's Bonni! I am so excited to talk to you!"

The appointment I had been waiting for was here, and I completely forgot. Right away, hearing Bonni's voice, I felt at ease. It was a comfort I did not know I was even missing.

I apologized profusely because I was in the car with my children, and I had forgotten all about the appointment. She asked if I wanted to reschedule. "No, I've been wanting to talk to you."

As I took her off Bluetooth, she said in my ear, "So you just went through a major life event, seems like it was pretty traumatic. If you aren't ready to hear this, just let me know, but I would love to talk to you about your next relationship because that is going to be amazing."

I'm sorry, what? It had only been a month, and I was just starting to settle into the whole I-am-going-to-be-alone-forever phase of a breakup. This woman must be crazy—but I was very intrigued.

"No, I am serious—the great love of your life is around the corner. We can talk next time about it. I can sense you want to talk about what happened. Tell me about it."

I gave her the abbreviated version and talked in code since the kids were in the car. Thankfully, she understood. What she had said next to me was beyond comforting:

"You don't need me to say this to you, but you did the right thing. You and Don were not meant to be married forever. I know you are worried about the future and the kids. Your kids are going to be fine. If you had stayed with him, the lasting effects would be much worse for your children, particularly your son. I know you are worried about upcoming court stuff. It will all be okay. He won't face jail time, and I think you are on the fence with how you feel about that. You are strong, and it is okay if you tear up. Grab your sister's hand when you are in the courtroom, and she will help you get through it."

I understand that anyone, who hears what had just happened, could have come to the same conclusion. It was just something about the way she was talking. I told her how much our quick twenty-minute conversation had helped. I got off the phone and immediately made another appointment. There was one available for the following week that worked with my schedule. It was a sign, and her comfort was something that I definitely needed right then. I also wanted to hear more about how the great love of my life was just around the corner.

Bonni quickly became the person I turned to every Wednesday and still do. I should also note here that I have, now, a fabulous actual therapist, who, coupled with Bonni, have helped put me back together again. Thank you, Bethany and Bonni.

I realized Bonni was right. I was worried about the upcoming criminal hearing. I was petrified about having to get on the stand and relive that night, which I was told might happen. I did not want to have to do that in front of him or in front of my family. My father had taken this opportunity to invite my entire family to support me—and I mean my entire family. He meant well; he was trying to support me the best way he could.

The morning of the hearing, my sister, Tara, showed up at my house. I told her how worried I was about having to get on the stand. I also was feeling conflicted—I wanted him to pay for what he did that night and what he had done to me for ten years, but I also did not know if him going to jail was the best option for the kids. They had been through so much, and I didn't know if the thought of their dad in jail would be too much for them to handle.

Tara did what any good big sister would do. She handed me a bottle of tequila and told me to take a shot. "It will help calm your nerves."

Never one to disagree with her, or turn down tequila, I took the shot and stood in the kitchen with my family, working up the nerve to get in the car.

The tequila had not done the wonders I had hoped it would. I contemplated taking another shot but realized showing up to court with alcohol on my breath probably would not be the best choice.

My brother-in-law grabbed my arms before I walked out and said, "You lose your nerve. You remember one thing. That man threatened your kids. You can't let him do that again."

That was all I needed. I knew I could do this.

It turned out I did not need to worry about getting on the stand. As I was waiting in the Fairfax County Courthouse for the hearing to begin, I was pulled into a room with the Commonwealth attorney, my criminal attorney, the police officer who responded that night, the domestic violence detective, and the domestic violence advocate. It was a full house.

The Commonwealth attorney began to talk quickly, and I instantly wanted to punch him in his face. "Right, so he isn't going to face jail time. He's going to get the first offender disposition. Meaning, if he stays out of trouble for two years, it will go off his record. We will issue you a permanent protective order that is good for two years, and he will begin having supervised visits regarding the kids. Any questions?"

I'm sorry, what? He wasn't going to face jail time for what he did? Worst of all, if he was a good boy all of this would magically go away for him? This was not fair, not fair at all. I did not want him to go to jail, necessarily, but I did want him to pay somehow.

"So he has no real consequences?"

"No, he does. This is his first offense, so there isn't a lot we can do. He has supervised visits and you get a protective order, which will look good for the divorce and custody. You look upset, Ms. Lee," the Commonwealth attorney said.

You bet I was. I was infuriated. I had done everything I was supposed to do to protect my children and myself. Now, the people I was asking for help, whose job it was to help me, were doing nothing because I had not previously called the police.

"I am upset. This is bullshit. This is the reason most domestic violence victims don't come forward because they don't believe anything will happen."

I walked out right smack into my friends, who had showed up for support. I told them and my family that was there. Safety in numbers. We were all upset.

I sat through the hearing with my family and friends supporting me. Bonni was right, holding my sister's hand got me through it. Although, at times, I was holding her down from getting up to kill Don. At one point, my brother also whispered in my ear that it was a good thing he didn't know Don had threatened my son until this moment.

It did not take long. I got my protective order for two years. I walked out of the courtroom and took a deep breath. I needed a drink. I needed a girl's night. And I really needed to hear about how this great love of my life was about to walk in and sweep me off my feet.

Chapter 12:
London Calling

You know I love a London boy.
—Taylor Swift

"OH MY GOD, ALLYSON, HE'S hot! What did you say you do when you think someone is cute?"

"You swipe right, but seriously, Amanda, don't."

"Oops! I did. It says you can be a match—what do I do now?"

"You send them a message, but Amanda, don't, really."

"I just said hi. If he responds, just tell him it was your drunk friend." I handed Allyson back her phone and went back to our other friends and our fireball shots. I was having one epic girl's night and had just stolen my friend Allyson's phone to figure out how exactly this whole online dating thing worked.

A few minutes later, Allyson started laughing. "Your phone is going to buzz in a minute. It's him."

She was right, it was. Enter London.

He was the most handsome man I have ever laid eyes on, both in pictures and in real life. What struck me, even in my slightly inebriated state, were his kind eyes. And there was also something about his face; it felt like I already knew him. He has brown hair, dark eyes, and a beard. He looked like Adam Levine, except hotter.

We texted that night and throughout the next week. He was just moving to Virginia, and we agreed to meet the first Friday after he got settled.

I almost did not go. I told Sue how nervous I was.

"I'm not going."

"Don't be ridiculous. Get an Uber and go!" Sue pleaded with me. "It's too soon."

"Well, there is only one way to find out. Go. Text me from the Uber." Sue hung up. She was right: I needed to just go. Worst case scenario, I would get the first post-separation date out of the way.

I had the Uber ride from hell. My Uber driver drove on the grass at one point and went down a one-way street the wrong way. I was just praying I would make it to my date. I jumped out of the car a block early.

When I arrived, London opened his apartment building door. I had a moment where I couldn't catch my breath—at first, I thought it was just my relief from being out of the Uber, but I quickly realized it was him. The minute I saw him in person, I knew there was something there. I hugged him, and he introduced himself. Oh my god, is that an accent I detect? Yup, he's British.

I was nervous, and so was he, but we instantly hit it off. I had always thought love at first sight was utter crap, but I can tell you the exact moment I knew that I was going to fall for him, hard.

For our first date, we went out to a bar for drinks. At one point, he looked up as I walked across the room. We locked eyes and I knew. I knew that I was about to fall head over heels in love with this man.

If I was not completely sold at that moment, I was moments later when he kissed me. I've had a fair share of first kisses, but this felt different. When I pulled back and looked into his eyes, my fears that this might be happening too soon, just two and a half months after the traumatic events of August 3, faded away. My fear that I would never be able to trust or love another man faded away as well. I knew the man I was staring at was going to be in my life, and I could not be more excited. I was so confident that it never even occurred to me that he might not feel the same way.

We talked the next day and the day after that. We began to see each other once a week, then several times a week. I was in love with a London boy, and I could not get enough of him.

I decided that he was becoming a big part of my life and that it was time for him to meet the kids. He had been asking to meet them, and after only two months of dating it was soon, but it felt like the natural next step. If we were ever going to be together permanently, we needed to see how it worked with the kids.

One cold December Saturday morning, we pulled into my driveway following our "best friend sleepover," as Tessa called it. We decided he would come in to meet the kids. We were both nervous about taking this big step so soon, but it did feel right.

"Are you sure? This is a big step," he said.

"I know, but this feels right," I said.

"I agree."

When we walked in, the kids were still in their pajamas, eating breakfast. I told them both I wanted them to meet someone very special, who had brought chocolate. They were both excited to meet this "new friend."

My phone started buzzing. I ignored it at first, but when it kept going, I checked it. It was Don. We were only supposed to communicate about the children, something he kept forgetting. My lawyer had already had to threaten his lawyer with a trip to the Magistrate.

"I cannot believe you," his message said. The messages continued: "I am demanding to speak to the kids right now."

"How could you introduce another man to the kids so soon?"

"Way to confuse them."

I looked at my phone in disbelief. How did he know London and I were at the house together? Then, I realized: Don was watching me.

Chapter 13:
Things can Always be Worse

Never give up. Today is hard, tomorrow will be worse, but the day after tomorrow will be sunshine

—Jack Ma

I PUT MY PHONE BACK IN my pocket and tried to enjoy the morning, but I couldn't. I was unnerved; he was somehow watching me, but how? Were their cameras inside the house I did not know about? Outside of the house? When he lived there, Don had set up some cameras both inside and outside the house, but at the instructions of the police officers, I had disconnected and taken them all down. Maybe I missed one?

When London left, I went over to Jackie and Jackson's house and asked Jackson what he thought I should do. As we were discussing my options, my phone buzzed again. It was Don.

"Why is our daughter running around outside without a coat on? It's thirty degrees outside?" he typed.

I froze and showed Jackson my phone.

"Type exactly what I say," Jackson instructed. "Write 'stop stalking me.' It's important you use those exact words."

I did just that, and then, there were no more messages. Jackson told me to email my attorney right there and then, which I did. The three of us tried to figure out how he was watching—it had to be an outside camera.

I was scared. Was it not enough that this man had abused me for ten years?

I firmly believe, and to this day, that Don enjoys scaring me. Over the course of our marriage, he got some sick, twisted joy knowing what he was doing was frightening me. It was a way for him to control what I was doing, and he had lost that control that night I finally stood up to him. Watching and harassing me was his way of trying to control me yet again.

That night I triple-checked to make sure my new state-of-the-art alarm system—which was costing me a fortune—was on and then slept with my high school field hockey stick next to me.

I spoke to my attorney the next day. She told me to make sure I document everything that happened and that she wanted me to get the house swept by a private investigator. I made an appointment for Friday.

When London was last at the house, the kids had invited him over for dinner that Wednesday. The messages had stopped since I told Don to stop stalking me, and I thought that maybe that had been enough. Still, I wanted to be extra safe, so I had London park in the garage when he came for dinner that Wednesday.

He had just walked through the door and said hello to the three of us when my phone buzzed. It was him: Don.

"Please stop exposing our children to your boyfriend."

I ignored it, but he continued: "I cannot believe that you let him park in the garage."

I stared at my phone. How did he know London was here? How did he know he was in my garage? Tears started streaming down my face; I could not believe the amount of fear that I was feeling at that moment.

I showed London the messages and texted my neighbor, Jackson, what was going on. London held me. "You don't have to do this alone anymore," he said in my ear. "We are a team."

It was comforting and had it been said under different circumstances, I would have appreciated it. But I was too distracted.

Jackson had a different approach. "What the fuck! You need to call the cops. This is stalking."

Jackson and Jackie were both urging me to call the police, but I hesitated. I did not want to call the police while the kids were both awake. It had been traumatic enough for them just a few short months ago. I didn't know what the right move was at the moment, I just did not want to scare my children any more than they already were.

I tried to put the messages out of my mind. I blocked Don, both on my phone and in my head. I was determined to have a nice evening with my new boyfriend and the kids. I was going to remember this night with happy memories—and I do.

After I tucked the kids in, London pulled me into the kitchen. In between kissing me, he started telling me just how amazing he thought I was. Then, he held my face in his hands and told me loved me. Bonni was right: the great love of my life had officially entered the picture.

The next day, Bonni instructed me to look at my neighbors' house for cameras. "He has access to one of their cameras," she said. "Go look around at your neighbors' houses and see if anyone has a camera pointing directly at your house."

My neighbors? No way. I lived in a small seven-house cul-de-sac. Everyone knew what had happened. Surely someone would not give Don access to one of their cameras. Maybe they did not agree with me divorcing him, but there really was no getting around the fact he had threatened my life.

When the private investigator showed up, I had to giggle. He looked like he was auditioning for a role in *Ghostbusters* with the amount of gear he had on—except he was about one hundred pounds over the weight limit. He looked at everything inside and out, as well as all the electronics and my car. He did not find anything. As he was leaving, he wished me luck and said, "I hope I don't see you on the news one day."

I did not know what to say to that, so I did a nervous laugh.

I followed the plan and called the non-emergency number and asked that a police officer come to the house. A female officer showed up, and I thought I had hit the jackpot. Obviously, a female officer would be more sympathetic to me than a male, sisterhood and all.

I was wrong. As soon as I opened the door, I could tell she was annoyed that she was the one being called out to my house. The look on her face was one of utter irritation. She clearly did not want to be there and told me she could do nothing about a neighbor who had a camera pointed at my house. As long as it was on their property, they could point a camera anywhere they wanted. This was also not a violation of the protective order either.

I was a stunned. How? The man is stalking me and texting me about it. But I did not have a clause in the protective order stating that he could not surveil me; therefore, it was not a clear violation. She suggested I go back to court to get that added. The most that she could do was file a police report. I said fine and looked hopelessly at Jackie, who had come over for moral support. I felt like once again he was getting away with murder.

I called my attorney, and we set a court date to get the stalking clause added to the protective order. She told me to start bracing myself because the next step was to start trying to work out details of the divorce—and that was bound to get even worse.

Chapter 14:
The Mother-in-Law

Adam and Eve were the happiest and
the luckiest couple in the world, because
neither of them had a mother-in-law.

—Unknown

WHEN I FIRST GOT ENGAGED, I thought I had hit the jackpot when it came to mothers-in-law. Helen was young (she had Don in her early twenties), into yoga, a wine drinking buddy, and a sympathetic ear to the anger I endured. Don's father, in contrast, had a very similar temperament to his. While I never got the full details, I suspect that he (and still is) verbally abusive to her.

Helen was the one I called when I needed advice on how to deal with Don and his anger. She was the one I called when things got too much. And she was the one I called when I needed someone to intervene and try to help him.

I learned, not very quickly, that the help I so desperately thought I was receiving from her was never going to come. When she told me that she would call the cops on her own son should he ever come after me again, I thought she was my safe person. She told me that she would talk to Don, and have his dad talk to him, and that they were going to try and get him help. She would say this to me over and over again. No help ever came until after the events of August, and by that time, it was too late.

I remember the exact moment that I realized that while she may always sympathize with me, she never will be the safe person

I thought she was. It was the day before Christmas Eve, when the kids were two and one. We had our hands full, to say the least, and traveling with two small children was extremely stressful. The three-hour drive up to Pennsylvania that day was not pleasant, with both children crying most of the way.

We had gotten to her house, and Don was extremely on edge. We began to argue about something trivial. I was standing next to Ethan, trying to get the TV to work. Don was so mad about, well, everything, that he hit my arm so hard the remote went flying across the room. A full-on swing that left a welt on my hand. And he did this in full view of both the children and his parents.

I took one look at him, one look at our children's scared faces, and decided I was going to drive to my sister's house that night. Tara lived only about forty-five minutes from my in-laws. Don stormed off when I announced my plans, and his father begged me to stay, reminding me it was Christmas and that his son was truly sorry. Helen took a different route.

"Well, Amanda, it is your choice. It is your choice to break apart your family tonight."

I remember staring at her blankly. Isn't it the person who is doing the abuse the one breaking the family apart, not the one who was leaving? Still, her words stung. I looked back at the kids, who were happily playing at the moment, and decided to stay.

She would utter a similar phrase to me the last time we spoke on the phone—August 4, the day after. This time she said to me, "Your choices and your decisions will affect all of us."

I did not respond, not because the words stung, but because I had no response. I could care less if she was upset. My concern was the safety of myself and my children.

Helen and I did not speak for several months. It was right before Thanksgiving that she called me on my way to work—I still regret picking up the phone instantly. Don had just been told he needed to have emergency open heart surgery. Because the two of us were restricted about what we could speak about, he told me that his mother would be the one to contact with any questions. I did not want to speak to her. When she called, I was not sure exactly what to expect.

I was met with anger. The first thing she did was tell me she wanted to see the kids that coming weekend. I was fine with that, but then, she started attacking me and wanted to know why I had not called her.

I was a little dumbstruck. Why would I call her? Her son had just threatened to kill me, and the last phone conversation we had was not exactly the most sympathetic. When I told her this, she accused me of keeping her away from the kids.

"I told you, Amanda, your choices and your decisions will affect all of us," she said again.

I interrupted her when she started talking about the support she needed to get through this. "I'm sorry," I said, "but I don't give a shit about the support you need. I care about these two little kids, and if you truly cared, you could have reached out. I am the victim here. Your life was not threatened, mine was. I did not turn my back on you. You turned your back on me." And then, I hung up.

She texted me a few hours later, saying she was emotional because she just found out Don needed heart surgery. She said she was here for me if I had any questions. I ignored it. She texted a few days later, saying she still wanted to see the children. I agreed, which was my second mistake.

Helen came over on a Friday evening after the kids and I came home from school. She had brought pizza, which Tessa loved and Ethan refused to eat. The kids were excited to see her, at first. They always had a great relationship.

About a half hour into her visit, I looked at Ethan's face and saw something was wrong. He looked at me and told me his belly hurt and that he wanted to go to his room—that was his code for when he was upset. Having her in the house was getting to be too much for him, and he needed to escape. My heart broke instantly.

She told me she had a few things she needed to gather for Don, and I told her she could do that when the kids went to bed. This did not make her happy, but I did not care. I felt like the last thing the kids, particularly my son, needed to see was their grandmother hauling their father's stuff out of the house.

Boy, did she take stuff—her list was two pages long! I did not fight her on any of it; it was just stuff and I was glad to be rid of it.

As she was gathering the last bit, she stopped me right at the basement stairs.

"Amanda, I need to ask you something. I just went into the safe, and I saw that the money that used to be there is no longer there. What happened to it?"

"You went into my safe?" I was in disbelief.

"Yes, where's the money?"

"Well, the first issue is that you went into the safe, but I will deal with that later. Are you talking about the money that I did not know about? That money was used."

"What did you spend it on?" She asked, barely containing her anger.

"None of your business."

"Well, Amanda, that was just really unkind of you. That is money he had been saving from his grandmother."

"I'm sorry, did you just say it was unkind? You have some balls. You are standing at the exact same spot your son did when he got a gas can and threatened to burn the house down with our family in it!"

I could not hold it back. I was yelling at her. I could not believe her audacity, telling me that I was unkind when it was her son who had abused me for all these years. And it was she who used to be the sympathetic ear on the phone.

She held up her hand in front of her face and told me to "pipe down" because my children were in the house. I immediately told her to get out.

"You know, Amanda, I'm not excusing what he did or saying it was right."

"That is exactly what you are doing. If that is what you and your family need to do so you can sleep at night, then so be it. But you will never again do it under my roof."

At this moment, Tessa came down. Not wanting her to hear or be a part of this conversation, we both stopped talking to each other as she continued to load her car.

As she left, she touched my arm. "Good luck in your new life, Amanda." She then walked out the door.

I walked my daughter upstairs to her room, then went into mine and burst into tears the minute I shut the door. I never expected her to take my side, but I also never expected to get the gaslighting I did from her. I made a different life decision than she did: she chose to stay, keeping the family together at all costs. I could point fingers and say perhaps her staying was the reason Don turned out the way he did, but I don't know that for certain. What I did know is that she clearly thought this was my fault. And that realization hurt like hell.

Chapter 15:
Things Got Worse...

Courage is being scared to death…
and saddling up anyway.
—John Wayne

D ON HAD EMERGENCY OPEN HEART surgery in the beginning of January, and that put everything to a standstill, including his supervised visits with the children. He retreated to Pennsylvania to recover at his parents' house, and I tried to look at this time as a chance to breathe.

He was scheduled to resume his visits with the kids in March, but the day of his first visit with them was abruptly cut by the Governor of Virginia—the entire state and country was shutting down due to the pandemic. This effectively put an end to all of his visits, and to our divorce proceedings as well.

He did still see the children on FaceTime calls every other night. I clearly was not thinking when I agreed to this. At first, it was good for the kids, and now with them unable to see their father due to a global pandemic, it was, at least, a way for them to stay connected with him.

For me, however, they were torture. I heard his voice every other day; it was awful. At first, I tried not to be in the same room when the calls were happening, but anyone who has ever FaceTimed with two small children knows it is normally a disaster. The kids spent more time fighting with each other than they did actually speaking to him.

We all tried to make the best of it and rearrange schedules to accommodate it, and I vowed to make sure every-other-day-FaceTime calls were not part of the final custody agreement.

With Don back in the area, I started waiting for my child support to appear again. We had reached an agreement that while he was out of work and recovering, his support payments could be paused, but now, he was officially back to work. I kept checking my account.

I was doing fine financially—actually, this was the best I had done financially in a long time. I no longer had him buying things and then demanding I pay half since it was "shared." I had budgeted well for these few months, but we were now past that time period.

My attorney was desperately trying to get a hold of his attorney, to find out what was going on with child support.

"Something does not seem right," she kept saying to me.

It turns out, the reason his attorney was not getting back to mine was because she had fired him. To be honest, I had no idea this was even something attorneys did. I assumed it was because he was difficult to deal with. There was a different reason, however.

"I still think something is up with these payments," my attorney was saying to me after we found out he was on the hunt for new representation. "I'm going to start subpoenaing his employment history and pay stubs."

The process took several weeks, but she found out that he was, in fact, paid the entire time he was recovering. He had lied; he had withheld money to support his children. I know he did it to hurt me, and it infuriated me to no end. "I guarantee this was the last straw for his attorney," my lawyer said.

We spent the summer going between his new attorney—who liked to paint me as someone who was sleeping with half of Northern Virginia—and my attorney to try and settle custody. We reached an agreement at the end of August.

I did my best to try and put my personal feelings aside and do what was best for the children. They resumed visits with him in May and were enjoying seeing him again. I insisted we start slow and that there were mental health checkpoints that he had to maintain. Now that he had an anger management coach, life coach, psychiatrist, and had found Jesus, I figured he would be able to easily provide those.

The last thing to untangle was the financial settlement. I knew that this was going to be the one he dug his heels in for, even more so than custody. Don is very materialistic, and I think part of the reason he was first attracted to me was because I come from a family with money.

He was granted six hours in our marital home to "survey" his personal property. I was not allowed to be there due to the protective order, nor did I want to be there. I hired a private investigator to be there on my behalf.

The year prior, I was given exclusive rights to the house, and I had been trying to create a new life for myself and the children. I tried to erase all aspects of him from the home, with the exception of the pictures I placed in the children's bedrooms. When I glanced at a picture of London, myself, and the children on my fireplace mantel, I realized that he was going to trash the house and go through every single thing he could find.

Don's morning came. I greeted the private investigator at the door, wished him well, and left for the day. I turned my alerts off for my cameras outside. I did not care to have my phone buzz throughout the day, notifying me he was walking around the property.

What happened next was so much worse than I ever imagined. When I arrived home, the private investigator informed me that Don has anger problems—no kidding. He told me how he literally went through every drawer we owned, including my underwear drawer. Don freaked out about all the good alcohol that I drank (totally did that on purpose), the money in the safe (yup, spent every last dime), and a pregnancy test.

"A pregnancy test?" I asked.

"Yeah, he said he found a used pregnancy test with urine still on it," the investigator told me. I knew that one was a lie. There were no used pregnancy tests. I thanked the investigator for his time, but his parting words sent a chill up my spine:

"You need to be careful. He's smart, and he's dangerous."

The next day, as I was teaching from home, I remembered that I had not turned my alerts for the house alarm back on. As I opened the app for my alarm system, I noticed something was not right—all the cameras were down, and there was an alert saying that the Smart Gateway was malfunctioning. I immediately texted my service guy, James, with the alarm company to tell him that Don was in the house the previous day and that all of the alerts popped up.

"Oh, he definitely messed with it," he wrote back.

"Really, you think so?"

"Oh yeah. When the Smart Gateway malfunctions, that means if the alarm goes off, it won't notify the police or fire department. No way that is done, and all the cameras are done by coincidence. I'll be over in a few hours to fix it."

I collapsed on the kitchen floor. This could not be happening. I felt violated the day before when I found out he went through my underwear drawer, but this was different. He was messing with my safety, and it scared me. I was shaking when I received an email from my attorney.

Don had decided the month prior that he was going to accuse me of adultery. He had it in his head (and probably still does) that London and I started seeing each other while Don and I were still married. My attorney told him to prove it. I was about to read how he knew I was in a relationship with London.

The email contained video footage from my neighbors' house, from a camera that was directly pointed at my house. In addition to the footage, there was a private investigator's report with dozens of photos of London and I holding hands, hugging, and kissing.

I had never felt so violated. I collapsed onto the floor and called London. He was the comfort that I needed. "Look at it this way, what a great way for us to look back at some of our favorite moments," he said. God, he is amazing.

When James came over that night to fix the alarm, he discovered that Don had tried to break into the alarm system as well. Don had tried to redirect all the cameras to his phone, but when that did not work, he wiped the cameras.

I called Jackson and asked him to come over to advise me what to do. "Tomorrow, we are going to the magistrate and pressing charges. I will help walk you through this," he said.

I said okay. James fixed what he could with the cameras and the alarm system. I felt better but still could not sleep. The next morning, I was going into the magistrate and asking them to press charges and arrest Don. Again.

Jackson walked me into the magistrate and helped me through what I needed to say. I rehearsed it several times before it was our turn, but I was so nervous. I wasn't nervous because I didn't think they would believe me. I was sad that I was in this position once again. I couldn't stand still while we waited and kept fidgeting the entire time.

When the magistrate handed me the paperwork, Jackson helped me fill it out too. I was shaking when I handed it all back to the magistrate. It took them all of five minutes to tell me that they would file charges and gave me a court hearing date for the following February.

Don found out about the charges the following week and was arrested when the warrant was served.

Chapter 16:
And Then, He Cheated

I dug my keys into the side of his pretty
little souped-up-four-wheel-drive.
—Carrie Underwood

IT TOOK ME LONGER THAN I let on to fully let London into my heart. I was scared. I was scared he was going to hurt me and my children. He convinced me to let him in. We would sit for hours upon hours, and he would tell me what a beautiful life we were going to have. After a while, I started to believe him. I let him in.

London started calling Ethan and Tessa, "our babies" and started saying he wanted to marry me. To be honest, I wanted to marry him. I wanted to create a family with him. I wanted to have more children and them to be half him and half me. I kept jokingly asking how we could get them to have little British accents.

That summer, we started looking at houses together. He was going to buy us a house to start our family in. He used to say he was going to build me "a nest." A safe place for me to rest my head.

It was right around Tessa's birthday when I found out. When I found out he had cheated on me.

I was lying in bed one night when I received a Facebook message from a person I did not know. He told me that I needed to talk to my man and that London was cheating on me. I immediately sent the message to London who called me right away. Yes, he had drinks with a female coworker, but that was it. I believed him. I had no reason not to. I went to bed that night not thinking too much of it.

The next day while driving home from my friend Candice's house I received another Facebook message. This time from London's coworker. It simply read, "I slept with him. Sorry."

I had to read it a few times. I took a screenshot and again, sent it directly to London. He called me immediately. I will never forget that day. That moment looking into his eyes. I knew then that he wasn't telling me everything. He looked at me and said that we needed to talk. That something did happen. She had stayed over, but they only kissed.

I hung up on him. To be fair, I hung up on him several times in the span of a few minutes. I yelled, I cried. He cried. He begged me to stay. I was thirty seconds away from kicking him to the curb when he said the thing that got me. He told me that he feels the way about me that his father does about his mother. I looked into his eyes and decided right then and there I was going to believe him and work things out.

And we did…for about a month. He showered me with affection, we even found a house that we both loved. He put an offer in on the house, and it was accepted. We were on our way to creating our safe space, and I was determined to push the cheating out of my heart.

It had worked too, until October. London had come to visit, and we were just sitting down to dinner when the messages started again. The account was fake, I knew that much at this point, but was still pointing out that he was cheating on me. I also knew who was behind the fake Facebook account…Don. He had given one too many clues giving himself away. Like all things I had learned, he gave just enough away that I knew it was him but not enough that I could do anything about it. I was furious that he found out, and I was even more mad at London for giving him this kind of ammunition against me.

I could see the panic look on his face. I was stunned. We went upstairs to talk. I pressed him over and over again if he had slept with her. He finally admitted. Yes, he did have sex with her. It was one time.

I lost it. I cried hard. I could not believe he not only cheated on me but that he lied to me. I let him stay. In hindsight, I should not have. I was mad and hurt. I needed space, but taking space from someone has always scared me.

The next morning, he admitted that it had happened more than once. I was devastated. This man in front of me. This man I wanted to spend the rest of my life with had hurt me. The one thing I was so fearful of happening had happened, he had broken my heart into a million pieces.

I did not know what to do. So I stayed. I let him stay. I pushed the feelings deep down inside and decided to believe him. I believed that he was sorry, that it would not happen again. This was a matter of him being scared, not lust (although that did play a part). I forged on because there was only one clear reason to continue to forge on—I loved him.

Chapter 17:
Holy Crap, I'm Pregnant!

All that she wants is another baby.
—Ace of Base

"DO MY BOOBS LOOK BIG to you?"

I dragged Jackie into my kitchen and flashed her—the perks of living next door to one of your best friends.

"Um, yeah, they are huge! Is it because..." Jackie started and stopped.

"Pretty sure I am. I'm so nauseous and exhausted. And my nipples are huge and really hurt."

"Oh my god."

Oh my god was right. I thought I was done having children after Tessa, though not necessarily because I did not want any more children. Because I did not want to have any more children with Don.

On my second date with London, we started joking about having babies. We had never been super careful, and there had been a few close calls. I should not have been as shocked as I was, standing in my kitchen telling Jackie I was ninety-five percent sure I was pregnant.

"Take a test," Jackie urged me.

"It's way too soon. I need to wait at least another week," I said.

I've had two babies; I know what it feels like to be pregnant. I knew I was pregnant, there was no way around it.

I drove out to see London, who had moved nine hours away for work. As a surprise, I drove a U-Haul with all of his furniture to his new house. He had been saying he needed to get his stuff, and so I booked a small truck, even though I had never driven one before in my life and enlisted a few friends to help put the furniture in, and was off.

I was determined not to tell London until I took a test; I did not want to freak him out, or worse, excite him and then disappoint him. I had taken a test the night before my drive, but it was positive, then negative, then went blank. I figured it was a faulty test, but Jackie said to me, "A positive is a positive."

We had a blissful weekend that weekend. He was so appreciative of the fact I drove everything out there for him. It was perfect, until Sunday morning.

I woke up with the worst nausea. I tried my best to hide that I was not feeling well, but my poker face has never been too good. So I looked at him, took a deep breath, and blurted out, "I think I am pregnant."

Then, I burst into tears.

If there was ever a perfect boyfriend response to what I just said, it was this. He held me, told me he loved me, and that everything was going to be okay. He reassured me that this was not a bad thing and that we would figure it out together, as a team.

I called my doctor the Monday I got back. She told me that the only way to be sure I was pregnant was to take a test or come in for a blood test. I had to wait until several days after my missed period for both of my children and figured I should do the same. The doctor said it was up to me. "Amanda, you've been pregnant. If you want to wait that is fine; however, if you are having these symptoms and you are sure, then treat yourself like you are pregnant and take care of yourself."

I bought prenatal vitamins, cut out alcohol (I couldn't really stomach it at that point anyway), cut back on caffeine, and tried to rest and take it easy as much as possible.

I waited until the day I knew it was close enough to my period that I might get a positive result. It was twelve days before Christmas, and I could not wait any longer. It was positive.

I cried. I knew, at that moment, that I wanted this baby; I wanted a piece of London and me. I immediately went online to and bought a onesie that said I love my Daddy and planned to give it to London on Christmas morning. We had already been texting several times a day about potential baby names and what our future would look like. I could not wait to see the look on his face.

That night, I woke up with severe cramps. "Something's wrong," I said out loud. The only other time I had experienced something like this was during labor. That is what it felt like, the early stages of labor.

I looked at the clock: 2:30 a.m. I ran to the bathroom. There was blood. Lots of blood. The sheer amount of it, and the cramping, were scary. I knew what was happening. I was having a miscarriage. I was losing the baby.

I waited until 6:00 a.m. to call London. I did not want to wake him up with this news. If I am being honest, the real reason was that I was trying to get up the courage to tell him. I knew he was nervous about a baby, but I also knew more than anything that he was excited. I was also in an immense amount of pain and dealing with a lot of blood.

I started crying as the phone was ringing. He picked up immediately. I do not remember what I said, but he told me I should not have waited to call, that he would be coming sooner, and that he loved me.

I hung up and looked around the room. "I'm having a miscarriage," I said out loud. I had to, hoping that it would help with the shock, because in exactly twenty minutes, I had to be up and downstairs. Being a single mom, I did not have time to have a personal crisis.

Looking back, I do not know how I was even functioning that morning. I somehow managed to get the kids up, dressed, fed, and to school all on time. I was running to the bathroom to deal with the blood quite a bit and told the kids I was not feeling well as an excuse for how slowly I was moving. I taught from my couch, the only day I was happy for virtual school.

I texted Jackie, who immediately offered to come help. I appreciated it, but I declined. Not because I did not need help but because

I wanted to be alone. I cried more that day than any day before. I cried because I had lost something. I cried because I felt like I had been through enough. I cried because I was alone. I wasn't really alone; London was on his way, and I had a great support system. But I felt very alone all the same.

I also felt ashamed. Why couldn't I hold onto this baby? Did I do something differently this time than I did with my other two children? The simple fact was that I had no control over what was happening. I lost something I did not want to lose and that sucked, big time.

I called my doctor and spoke to a nurse. She scheduled an appointment for me and told me what I should do to make myself more comfortable at home, as well as all the scary things I should look out for. I hoped none of those would happen.

She told me to take a pregnancy test. If it was positive, they were going to want to see me that day. If it was negative, I could wait. It was negative. I cried even harder.

When I went into the office, the doctor confirmed what I already knew: it was a miscarriage. No, it was not due to anything that I did or didn't do. Yes, being over thirty-five put me in a greater risk category. He told me it was better to miscarry now than after hearing the heartbeat. I was doing a pretty good job of holding it together in the exam room, but that last statement stung. I was never going to be able to hear the baby's heartbeat.

I am a firm believer that everything happens for a reason. I do not know why that baby left my body, but it did. And it still breaks my heart to think about.

Chapter 18: Rock-Bottom

You know what's great about hitting rock bottom?
There's only one way left to go, and that's up!
—Matthew McConaughey, *Sing*

WHEN LONDON CAME, I WAS a mess. I was a mess before he came but an even bigger one now. I could not stop crying. The pain had gone away for a bit, but the cramping, when it came back, was awful. My body just ached.

I kept staring off into space. I had not slept and just felt very lost and alone, even with London sitting next to me.

"Are you okay?" he would ask me.

It was hard to look at him. It was hard to look into his eyes. His eyes that were so reassuring the last time we had seen each other, telling me that everything was going to be okay and that he was excited about the idea of a baby. I felt like I broke his dream. I felt like I broke us.

"I lost our baby," was always my response, followed by tears.

He said and did all the right things in the days following the miscarriage. We put on a brave face for the kids and tried to all get into the Christmas spirit. It was a tall order. We were spending Christmas in a place that made me (and London) uncomfortable, and for the first time ever, I had to share Christmas with Don.

The marital residence that I still called home did not evoke happy memories. If I was not looking around, remembering the places where abuse took place, I was constantly worried about being watched.

Every time I walked out the front door, I looked to the left, and there was the camera. While I doubted, at this point, that Don was still watching, it was still there. I had thought that my neighbors would have taken the camera down after my attorney subpoenaed the shit out of them for every communication they had with Don, but they did not.

Needless to say, it was not my first choice of locations to spend Christmas. But like before, I put on a brave face for the kids, who still called this house home and their safe spot.

Like most divorced couples, we tried to split Christmas as evenly as possible, rotating Christmas morning. I had them that first year Christmas morning, which was good because I do not know if I could have handled not being with them. Christmas morning is the big one to me, and I was already not looking forward to the next year when he would have them.

This year, I knew my time was limited with them. It would be just a few short hours, and then, they would be off with Don. The thought of that was killing me, on top of the pain I was already feeling about the miscarriage. And it was just as painful as I thought it would be.

London went back home a few days after Christmas. I was going to follow him the day before New Year's Eve, as Don had the kids on New Year's this year. My decision to fly was probably not the best on my already high anxiety, but one hour in the air beats nine in the car when you are trying to get somewhere fast.

As I said before, I'm not scared of flying—I'm scared of crashing. I am also very claustrophobic—not the best combination when traveling by airplane. I take a Xanax, and I am fine by takeoff, with just a little grip of the seat when I hear or feel something I deem unusual.

I knew I had two pills left for flying this time, and then, I would need to go back to see my physician. Except I could not find them, anywhere.

I tore the house apart. Nothing. I stood in my bedroom with my hands on my hips and figured what was the worst that could happen? Things were already awful.

I made it to see London safely, even though I thought I was going to die several times in flight. We had flown through a storm, never a fun thing for a nervous flier.

We had a blissful couple of days together. It was the first time in the past few weeks I had genuinely smiled. I think we both felt like we had reconnected after a pretty stressful time. Until the last night.

To say we had a big fight is an understatement; it was huge. We both said things that we did not mean. I lashed out at him; it was easier to be mad at him then myself. I was mad at myself and mad that I was not able to hold onto our baby. We almost lost each other that night, but thankfully, we did not.

When I got on the plane the next morning, I was devastated by our fight. I knew it was just an argument and that we were going to be fine, but I was still upset. I cried the whole plane ride home. This time, it was not from fear of crashing.

When I got home, I cried for another solid twenty-four hours. At times, I did not even know what I was crying about. I thought maybe I had not fully processed losing the baby.

"That's not it," Bonni said to me the following Monday. "This is bigger than that. You haven't processed anything in the past year. You need a break, and you need to surrender to the universe."

Sometimes, when Bonni talks to me about giving it up to the universe or my guides, I shrug it off. I believe what she tells me and listen to most of her advice, but I think it is my east coast mentality that gets in the way at times. This time, I listened to every word she said.

"You are screaming for a break," she continued. She gave me some grounding activities to practice. I knew I needed to do something.

"I feel like I've hit rock bottom," I said.

"Oh, you are well past rock bottom."

I started to keep a schedule, literally listing out every hour of every day, so that I knew what I had to be doing. It was oddly calming and helped to keep me more present, especially when it came to the kids. As someone who loves a good to-do list, I enjoyed crossing off things throughout the day.

Bonni also told me I needed to do something physical. "Go for a run or do yoga," she suggested. I was not exactly in my best running shape, so that was out. I've tried yoga throughout the years, and I always end up with the same result: when I am supposed to be "quieting my mind," I am busy thinking about the thirty other things I need to get done at that moment.

I decided on walking. My mom and I used to walk when I was fresh out of college and newly working, still living at home. We would walk in the morning, and it was time we both really enjoyed. It was really quite calming. So I popped my ear buds in, put on what my kids would call "calming music," and went off on a thirty-minute walk.

I felt better instantly. It was a great way to just clear my mind.

Bonni also told me to do a guided meditation. This one I was not thrilled with, but I followed her directions because, as we both had realized, I was crashing. I found a fifteen-minute guided mediation on YouTube for anxiety. I did it for the first week, every day, and then sporadically when I could. It did help to calm the anxiety.

After a week of my new routine with my grounding activity, I felt better, both physically and mentally. I had realized that a lot of my anxiety and stress was because I had not yet begun to deal with my feelings involving the night of August 3 but also with the abuse that I had been a victim of prior to that. I also realized that Bonni was right. At some point, I needed to realize that I could not control everything and had to surrender to the universe. I had to trust that, at some point, everything would work out in my favor.

"I'm so proud of you!" Bonni exclaimed the following week. "There is still too much energy around you. We need to find another outlet for you. You tried knitting, that didn't work. I don't know, maybe write a book."

I did try knitting, and actually, I love doing that now. It is very relaxing to be doing something with my hands while watching TV with the kids or sitting in a virtual meeting. I have made a fair number of things for family and friends now, and my specialty is scarves. It really is the only thing I can knit.

Writing a book struck a chord with me. This is not the first time she had brought up the idea, and Bonni is also not the first person to suggest it. Anytime I talk to friends, at least one person states that I really should write a book. We have joked, at times, that even Lifetime would find my story too unbelievable to turn into a movie.

I filed the idea away and went on my day. The next day, I woke up, and I immediately understood what she meant. I had this energy that needed an outlet. Maybe starting to write might not be such a bad thing.

That night, when I went to bed, I started thinking about what I would name my book. At 2:00 a.m., after being woken by Tessa, I started planning out my chapters. By 8:00 a.m., I was sitting down at my computer, planning out how I was going to actually accomplish this task.

I started writing, and the words just started flowing out of me. Turns out, I did have a story to tell—my own. After every chapter, I felt like I was releasing the pain that I had been holding onto—for years, in some instances. I sent it off in a pink bubble, hoping to never feel the anxiety surrounding it again.

It worked. Writing and telling my story allowed me to release years of pain and anxiety. As I wrote, I slowly crept up from rock bottom, vowing to never return to that dark place again.

Chapter 19:
Still Standing...a Conclusion of Sorts

*I'm still standing / better than I ever did / looking
like a true survivor / feeling like a little kid.*
—Sir Elton John

I WISH I COULD SAY THAT writing this book was my magic cure
all. Everything fell blissfully into place, and I am now living in a
cloud full of rainbows and unicorns (if only, Tessa would be so
excited). That did not happen.

London and I tried everything to make it work, but in the end,
we parted ways.

There's an old saying that goes something like this: there are
three sides to every story—yours, mine, and the truth. Well, this was
my truth. I am sure Don has a whole different version as to what happened both the night of August 3 and beyond. I am sure his mother
does as well. Actually, I know they do. That is fine; their truths are
what get them through the day, mine is what gets me through mine.
Deep down, we both know what transpired before, during, and after
our marriage.

Forgiveness can be a beautiful thing. It can free you from the
negative thoughts and anger you feel toward someone. And just
because you forgive, does not mean you forget the pain that you
went through.

I have worked hard over the past few years to forgive Don.
Forgive him for the years of our turbulent marriage and the traumatic events of that fateful night in August. I have forgiven him, and

I am working at trying to forgive the pain that August 3 brought on our children.

I used to wish I could forget. I so desperately always wanted to forget the pain that his verbal, and at times physical, abuse caused me. I wanted to erase the sound of his voice calling me those evil names and damaging my self-worth.

Until I realized that the pain is what has made me who I am. That pain has made me stronger. It has made me more of a badass than I already was.

I've learned a lot through my experience. I will never ever let anyone damage my self-esteem or that of my children's the way Don did. Heaven help anyone I feel is being harmful to my children in the future. And I will never again apologize for the person that I am or for who my children are.

I've also learned a lot about the legal system, especially in terms of what it means to be in a domestic violence "incident." In short, for survivors, the legal system sucks. I have felt like Don was seen as the victim and has been protected more than myself. That needs to change.

I am lucky. I had and have an amazing support system. Once my friends and family heard what was going on behind closed doors, they rallied around me. I also have amazingly generous parents, who not only helped me get on my own financial footing but also helped to pay the mounting legal bills.

Don and I still have a court appearance for when he broke into the alarm system. This will inevitably result in a trial, which will cost even more. We will also be in court again to file an extension of the protective order for another two-year span. While I have forgiven him, the fear of him and what he is capable of has not left me.

I think about the other women out there. I am not talking about other women that Don might have been sleeping with; I doubt there were any. I am talking about the other survivors of domestic violence. The ones who, like me, lived in a world of denial. The ones who think if they just love their partner a little more, the violence will stop. The ones who are not as lucky as I was and do not have the financial means to fight their abuser. Or the ones that are just too scared to leave.

I never imagined my life would turn out the way that it has. I never imagined I would be uttering the phrase, "Yes, I am a domestic violence survivor."

But here I sit and type, saying it over and over again. Yes, I am a domestic violence survivor. I am a survivor and that has made me stronger.

I am one of the lucky ones. I got away.

PS. For those of you wondering what happened to the $4,800. I spent it. Every. Last. Dime. I hired a personal shopper at Nordstrom's and pretended to be Julia Roberts in *Pretty Woman*. I spent four hours sipping champagne and having a blast with my dear friend, Candice. I told every single sales associate that I came in contact with that day what I was doing. When I left, I had eight bags and high-fived everyone on my way out. It felt damn good.

Acknowledgments

Holy shit, I wrote a book!

—AE Lee

THIS BOOK WOULD HAVE NEVER come to fruition without the push (more like shove) from my dear friend and spiritual guru Bonni. Thank you for the continued shoving in the right direction.

Thank you to my editor Megan Zavala who took my little pipe dream, fancied it up, and showed me that this could actually become reality.

Thank you to everyone at Fulton Books for taking care of my work as if it were their own words on paper. I will never be able to express my gratitude to everyone who has made this possible.

I would be remiss if I did not acknowledge the true heroes in my life, the ones that continuously pick me up and dust me off.

My parents who without their love and support, I shudder to think about where myself and my children would be. My entire family, for that matter, for the unconditional support that I have especially felt in the past few years. The incredible amount of pride that all of you felt for me for writing this book made me feel like I was back in the first grade in my leading role as one of the ugly stepsisters in *Cinderella*.

My Aldrin family, there are days that I did not know how I even got out of bed in the morning, let alone made it to work. Seeing and feeling supported by all of you during that time was how I was able to keep going. And while you did not know it at the time, the support transcended into me believing I could (and would) write this book.

To my amazing friends (you know who you are), from dropping everything right in the beginning, to coming with me to court
to just showing up at my house with doughnuts (and wine) and our
thirty-plus texts a night. Thank you. Thank you from the bottom of
my heart for being such amazing friends that extend far beyond what
I would ever imagine or be able to repay. How I would have gotten
through all this, let alone a pandemic, without all of you, is beyond
me. The support you showed for this book and for believing in me is
not one that I will ever be able to express.

Ethan and Tessa, while you are very young right now, someday
you will read this. I love you both, and while you don't realize it now,
you two are my constant inspiration.

And to all the survivors out there, in the immortal words of
Destiny's Child, "I'm a survivor, I'm gonna make it, I will survive,
keep on survivin'."

Keep on surviving.

About the Author

A. E. LEE STARTED HER career in Pennsylvania politics, and while she had hoped it would be everything like her favorite TV show, *The West Wing*, she quickly learned it was not. Long hours, little pay, and even less respect, she decided it was time for a change and embarked on a second career in education. She is now a beloved sixth-grade teacher in Fairfax County, Virginia.

She resides there, now, with her two beautiful children, Ethan and Tessa, where she continues her passion for writing and being a domestic violence advocate.

To view upcoming works or book A. E. Lee for speaking engagements, please visit www.authoraelee.com.

Cycling in & around Greater Manchester

Les Lumsdon

Published by Sigma Leisure – an imprint of
Sigma Press, 1 South Oak Lane, Wilmslow, Cheshire SK9 6AR, England.

British Library Cataloguing in Publication Data
A CIP record for this book is available from the British Library.

ISBN: 1-85058-476-1

Typesetting and Design by: Sigma Press, Wilmslow, Cheshire.

Cover photograph: Castlefield, Manchester (Chris Rushton)

Photographs: Chris Rushton

Maps: Jeremy Semmens

Printed by: MFP Design & Print

Contents

Cycle Manchester   1
   Bike Care   4
   Before your ride check: 4
   Before you Travel   5
   Travelling With Your Bike   6
   Where and Where not to Cycle   8

Cycling Further Afield   10

Traffic Free Rides   14

The Rides

Ride 1: Barrow Bridge   **25**
    Distance: *12 miles*

Ride 2: Bury   **29**
    Distance: *5 miles*

Ride 3: Chelford   **32**
    Distance: *15 miles*

Ride 4: Haigh Hall and Country Park   **37**
    Distance: *9 miles or 21 miles*

Ride 5: Heywood   **41**
    Distance: *5 miles*

Ride 6: High Legh   **45**
    Distance: *17 miles*

Ride 7: Manchester   **48**
    Distance: *2 miles*

Ride 8: Middlewood   **56**
          Distance: *8 miles or 15 miles*

Ride 9: Milnrow   **60**
                    Distance: *6 miles*

Ride 10: Mobberley   **64**
                    Distance: *8 miles*

Ride 11: Mossley   **67**
          Distance: *8 miles or 12 miles*

Ride 12: New Mills   **73**
                    Distance: *12 miles*

Ride 13: Patricroft   **77**
                    Distance: *6 miles*

Ride 14: Pennington Flash   **80**
                    Distance: *15 miles*

Ride 15: Rivington   **84**
          Distance: *8 miles to 10 miles*

Ride 16: Romiley   **89**
                    Distance: *6 miles*

Ride 17: Stalybridge   **92**
          Distance: *5 miles or 11 miles*

Ride 18: Stockport   **96**
                    Distance: *6 miles*

Ride 19: Tandle Hill   **99**
                    Distance: *5 miles*

Ride 20: Whaley Bridge   **102**
                    Distance: *12 miles*

Cyclists' Directory   **107**
   Useful Organisations   **107**

Useful Facilities   **111**
   Cycle Hire   **111**
   Cycle Holidays   **112**
   Cycle Shops   **112**

Cycle Manchester

The bicycle makes a very good companion, especially when in the countryside. There's nothing quite like it for those short distance explorations. The feeling of freedom, fun and fitness outweighs any minor hassles out there. It is not simply a matter of rolling out the miles to keep in trim; you really can get close to your surroundings on a bike. The views are better than from a car, the pace is more enjoyable and there's something very sociable about riding which is easier to experience than explain.

You are not on your own in thinking that the bike is OK, for the current estimate of cycle ownership in Britain is now over 20 million. Nor are cyclists just to be found down south or in East Anglia; the North West enjoys a higher ownership level of cycles per household than many other regions.

Despite the image presented in glamour cycling pictures found in the glossy magazines, most cycling is simply for everyday purposes such as journeys to work, to college or to the shops. But leisure cycling is fast becoming important again. Of all cycle trips approximately 40 percent are estimated to be for recreation. It will grow too as we become more leisure based.

Here's the rub. We would like to cycle more than we do now and would almost certainly cycle far more if things were different. This is precisely the case in Greater Manchester. Is it the weather? Surprisingly, recent surveys investigating the potential of cycling do not highlight the problem of weather. Although it rains a fair bit in the North West this is not the prime reason for leaving your bike at home.

You could also be forgiven for thinking that people dislike the idea of cycling because of hills – a factor that could be relevant around here, as Greater Manchester reaches into the very folds of the Pennines and that means exhilarating (or awful) climbs. But bikes now have far more gears (and lower gear ratios), so people are less worried about hills than previously. Yes, we still dislike hills but can manage them more easily with the new order of bike technology.

Cycle Owners

So what is it that makes us a nation of cycle owners rather than cycle users? In a nutshell . . . traffic. It is a greater inhibitor than all other factors put together. We simply hate sharing the road with the car. End of story for some. Place the book back on the shelf, but you'll miss out if you do.

The lot of the leisure cyclist is improving. Slowly but surely things are getting better and we have firm promises on which to build. Throughout the country there are many routes in the making for cyclists which are entirely off-road. Other schemes have combined quieter back lanes with some off-road sections. Back lanes themselves are equally pleasant if not better if cars can be kept at bay.

The North West is improving too. There is a long way to go but several district councils which make up Greater Manchester are planning and constructing more facilities for cyclists than before. Routes such as The Trans Pennine Trail, for example, involve well over 30 organisations and will offer great opportunities for the recreational cyclist when complete.

The Good, Bad and The Ugly

This book explains how you to get the best from such routes, many of which can be reached by public transport as well as by car. It describes the good, the bad and the ugly points about them, places to visit and so on. There's also a chapter about the Peak District, which brings together a catalogue of cycling opportunities for those who seek a day out or weekend in the countryside. Thanks to the efforts of Derbyshire County Council and the Peak National Park it is difficult to beat the Peak District in terms of the number of off-road cycle routes available.

If you have not cycled for some years or are currently not able to cycle, these are the routes to head for. Young and old, families and solo riders who enjoy a gentle saunter away from traffic will love them. In fact, on most Sundays throughout the year they are packed to near capacity with bikes so if you can travel on another day it could be even more enjoyable.

Very often it is not possible to make the time nor organise the travel arrangements to get out to the deepest countryside of Cheshire, northern Lancashire or the Peak District. You need routes closer to home, 5 to 10 mile runs suitable for afternoon or evening outings. Included are 20 such routes located in and around Greater Manchester. They are graded; several are easy rides mainly on back roads while others are more strenuous climbs on bridleways and tracks which are suitable for mountain biking. There's also an unusual little ride-cum-ramble featuring the historic splendour of Manchester and pausing at many of Manchester's famous statues. These enormous public tributes to people who were important in Victorian society are passed by daily without according much notice. Now is your chance to take a closer look.

Family cycling on the High Peak Trail

The National Cycling Centre

It would be remiss not to mention the sporting side of cycling and many clubs around Manchester organise trials and rides accordingly. Manchester is also home to Britain's purpose built velodrome which is bigger than most football pitches and contains a 250 metre cycle track made from Baltic Pine. The velodrome has a capacity for 3,500 seated spectators as well as numerous other facilities.

Bike Care

It is essential to maintain your bike in a roadworthy condition not only for the sake of safety, but also for a smooth ride and to prevent damage in the long run.

Before your ride check:

Your Brakes

The brake blocks must be correctly aligned with the wheel rims. Blocks and rims should be clean and free from oil or grease. The brake cable should be clear of any obstruction.

Your Chain

Chain, sprockets and chain-rings – make sure that they are clean of grit and dirt. Ensure that they are well lubricated so that gear changing is smooth.

Your Tyres

Clean out embedded pieces of stone or glass. Check that the side-walls are not damaged. Your tyres have to be pumped up hard.

Your Lights

If you intend riding at dusk lights are imperative for your own safety. Riding without lights is a sin not to be taken lightly.

All Parts

Before you go out check over the nuts and bolts of the bicycle to ensure that everything is tightened up.

Maintenance

Gone are the days when every cyclist was expected to spend hours maintaining his or her bike. If you are mechanically minded and have the right tools then basic maintenance is an easy and cheap option. There are several good books on the market.

If you are not mechanically minded and cannot cope with anything beyond the basics, take your bike into your local cycle dealer. Most will offer to service a bicycle to ensure that it is roadworthy and this need not be expensive. They also have the know-how and kit to undertake more fundamental maintenance when required such as replacing sprockets, bearings and brackets, chains, etc. Do not skimp on maintenance as a worn bike will give a much poorer ride and in time could well become dangerous.

Before you Travel

Before you set off it is essential to:

☐ check over your bike

☐ take a snack and drink

☐ make sure you have the right gear with you

Here's a check-list of what you should be wearing:

☐ Long sleeve shirt or blouse

☐ Jersey

☐ Leggings or loose trousers

☐ light waterproof

☐ trainers or cycling shoes

☐ helmet

And you should take:

☐ Puncture Repair kit including tyre levers

☐ Inner tube and pump

☐ All purpose spanner

☐ Loose change for phone!

☐   Bike lock

☐   Tissues to clean hands if repairs required

☐   snack and water bottle especially in hot weather

Taking this kit is essential. You are bound to have a puncture at some time, for it is the perennial curse of cyclists. Be prepared and you can fix a puncture in 15 minutes and be back on the road.

Travelling With Your Bike

The irony is that there is often less fuss and it can be cheaper to take your bike abroad with you by 'plane than to try to transport it to Cumbria or Staffordshire for the weekend. Sadly, the car is becoming the major transporter of the bike to the countryside; this is not surprising for, in recent years, British Railways have ignored demands from cyclists for a better deal. There is some evidence to suggest that the new rail companies will do differently – see below.

By Car

What we'd all like to do is to be able to cycle safely from home to the nearby countryside but there's not much chance of that at present. It could explain why the sales of bicycle racks for cars have soared. If you intend to use a strap-on carrier which fits to the rear of the car rather than a top rack, you must also purchase a number plate board (which can also display lights) to be fastened on top of the bikes. You might find that the police will stop you otherwise and advise accordingly. Newer models are coming on the market, however, which sit above the registration plates, and avoid the need for the board.

Carriers do have a good record. Those which convey cycles on the roof have been around longer but there are still fears that you might damage your bike by scraping the walls of low-level canal under-bridges, or on security bars at car park entrances, for example.

If you have a tow-bar it is possible to fix a tow-bar cycle carrier with ease. It avoids damage to the paintwork or straps loosening on rear strap-on carriers.

By Bus

Bus companies do not usually transport bikes. If you have seen one on board it is because of the kindness of the driver concerned in the given circumstances. This might be the case on the longer distance routes such as Greater Manchester South bus service 201 to Derby where the coach has a large boot. The carriage of a bike in this way is not ideal but when you're desperate to get home it is an option worth trying. Remember, carriage is at the discretion of the driver.

By Rail

Hats off to Greater Manchester Passenger Transport Executive and to Merseyside Travel. In the areas where they support train services you are entitled to take your bike on the train but are advised to avoid Peak hours. Guards might not be able to accept you if the train is very busy. That's the snag. In recent times the author has used trains to get to different parts of Greater Manchester and guards have willingly taken me and other cyclists on board.

The main problem lies with the trains themselves. They have limited space and generally no separate area for bikes. It is simply a matter of embarrassment between you and fellow passengers as they jostle by you to get in and out.

There have been attempts to allow more cyclists on trains in recent years. One is the Sunday service on the Hope Valley line, the other on the North Wales coast line where more trains convey larger guard vans. Merseyrail have also issued a superb booklet entitled "Rideabout", which features cycle rides from Merseyrail Stations.

Those seeking to take their cycle by train for longer distances will, believe it or not, have to check with each new train company. Companies with the InterCity identity tend to allow pre-booking of bikes on their trains at a flat fare, currently £3 per journey. The previous Regional Railways companies have a pre-booking system on some routes and at the discretion of the guard on others (where paying on the train is the norm). There are restrictions and these are published in a booklet.

To sum up, it is not easy to transport your bike by rail beyond the Greater Manchester boundary. The pity is that the train and cycle should be complementary and it would be really great if you could ride the train out to the countryside and pedal back.

Where and Where not to Cycle

Cyclists are losing friends because of a few thoughtless or discourteous riders who persist in riding on busy pavements at speed, down footpaths which are too narrow and where we have no legal right of way, or in pedestrian-only zones. Here's a run down of where you can cycle legally:

Public Roads

These come in all shapes and sizes with varying degrees of traffic, so choose your route carefully. Motorways are forbidden. Busy A and B roads should be avoided at all costs.

Unmetalled Roads

These routes are not maintained to a standard where they have a hard surface. They include County Roads and Roads Used As Public Paths (RUPPs) and By-ways Open To All Traffic (BOATs). It is hard to tell which is which but they are really attractive escapes from traffic.

Cycle Paths

These are surfaced routes alongside major highways such as the path to be found along certain parts of the A580 East Lancs Road. There are also permissive paths created by local authorities on disused railways, etc.

Cycle Ways

These are recommended routes which tend to use quiet back lanes and unclassified roads. The ways are very often way-marked such as The Cheshire Cycleway.

Bridleways

These are usually unsurfaced tracks, many hundreds of years old, on which walkers, horses and cyclists are permitted if not encouraged. Bridleways are usually signposted as such with a picture of a horse and rider.

Canals

Tow-paths are generally not available for cycling unless otherwise mentioned in the book. See the section on British Waterways.

Forests

Forest Enterprise has done much in recent years to open up forestry tracks to cyclists on a permissive basis. Some are rough, others smooth but they all offer great off-road cycling. In Greater Manchester we have to travel some distance to find such forests. The hope is that the new urban forest will offer scope for cycling.

Cycling Further Afield

For those considering a few days of cycling in the North West, there are several great opportunities.

Cheshire Cycleway

The Cheshire Cycleway is a 135-mile exploration of the county and it really does wind its way to all four corners. The best part is without doubt the very quiet back lanes south of Chester and through to Malpas, Wrenbury and Audlem. Here you can relax more. Other parts of the route hit far more traffic and cross busier main roads at dangerous places, for example, between Prestbury and Bollington.

In many respects the greatest joy of the route lies in the villages through which it passes, places such as Barthomley, Siddington, Marbury and Great Budworth and the number of attractions nearby. Those who dislike the hills should avoid the section between Prestbury and Fool's Nook as there are several climbs and descents, otherwise the Cheshire Cycleway is fairly and squarely on the level.

A leaflet is available from local tourist information offices which describes the route, places to visit and repair shops, etc. A small charge is made.

Cumbria Cycleway

This has to be a firm favourite of many a cyclist, for the 259-mile ride takes you to very varied countryside and generally away from the crowds that flock to the core of the Lake District. By far the best part is that through the Eden Valley, along quiet lanes which rarely see a visitor.

Other sections are extremely pleasant but involve main roads and through towns, such as in Furness to the south. The west coast has its charms – including such delightful villages as Duddon Bridge and Ravenglass – but the ride here involves longer sections of A and B roads and passes near the nuclear power plant at Sellafield.

The Cumbria Cycleway can be accessed by train easily, at places such as Dent or Garsdale on the Settle and Carlisle Railway, or Grange-over-Sands on the Barrow line from Manchester. It makes an ideal holiday for those who have some experience of road riding. A fold-out plan and information leaflet produced by Cumbria County Council is on sale at local tourist information offices.

The Cumbria Cycleway is now bisected by the C2C route from Whitehaven on the west coast to Sunderland on the east coast. This route is fairly hard going in places but offers an alternative cycle opportunity in Cumbria. There is a charge for the C2C route guide, which is available from Sustrans.

Lancashire Cycle Way

Promoted by way of a beautiful booklet, the Lancashire Cycleway is another county-wide ride of approximately 250 miles. It is really a combined northern and southern loop, meeting in the middle at Whalley. The booklet sets out the route in sections with clear maps and with a diagram showing the contours. You can see clearly where the hills are! There is also a solid amount of information on places to visit *en route*.

In many respects this one is not for less-experienced riders. While it follows many minor roads it still uses busy highways in places and they need to be treated with some degree of caution and experience. For example, if you are tempted to try the section from Rivington to Edgworth you have to ride along and make a right turn on the busy A606, which is decidedly unpleasant. The climbs can also be excruciating unless you are fit!

Don't be too harsh though, for there are cracking sections and very level ones, too, such as through the West Lancashire Plain. There are also wild and barely touched sections such as through the Trough of Bowland. The down-side is, as always the number of main roads to be crossed but, if treated with respect, the remainder of the ride should be up to the quality of the Lancashire Cycleway. Produced by Lancashire County Council, it is available from tourist information centres. There is a charge.

Mid Shires Way

The Mid Shires Way is a most unlikely route across Middle England from Stockport to Buckinghamshire. It is for walkers, cyclists and horse riders; one gets the impression that it is primarily for the latter user but on several sections it is suitable only for walkers.

The route is 225 miles long, linking the Trans Pennine Trail to the Ridgeway. Eventually it will join the proposed Pennine bridleway in the Peak District. The Mid-Shires Way should be an excellent route out to the Peak District for those who enjoy mountain biking on rough tracks. But at present it is not. This is frustrating, as it means that the most needed section for cyclists is missing. The Stockport to Compstall section is primarily for walkers – cyclists are not welcome beyond Vernon Park, although people do ride there. It is also impossible to ride through from Chadkirk to Etherow Country Park. From Marple onwards, the route becomes more viable to Buxton, then it is uncertain again.

There is far more work to be done before the Mid Shires Way attracts the cyclist and for that matter the horse rider out of Stockport. The route is way-marked with a double acorn and a folder with route descriptions is available.

Trans Pennine Trail

The Trans Pennine Trail, from Liverpool to Hull, and potentially offering a longer route from Ireland through to the Netherlands, is definitely in the making. The idea developed from an evaluation of many of the disused railways in Barnsley and someone felt it was time to link up similar old lines across the Pennines. The Trans Pennine Trail is still in progress for some sections are still under construction and others are currently for walkers only.

When the gaps are filled it will be an excellent way to enjoy cycling from home. Access will be available all along the route from Altrincham, Sale, Didsbury, Stockport and Hyde. For example, you will be able to cycle to Southport for the weekend or take a week's break by cycling through to the East Coast or Holland. What a brilliant idea!

You can join in the progress by contacting the Friends of the Trans Pennine Trail at the Department of Planning, Barnsley Metropolitan Borough Council, Central Offices, Kendray Street, Barnsley, S70 2TN.

West Yorkshire County Cycle Route

A 150-mile circular route around West Yorkshire which is mainly on minor roads and a very few sections of bridleways. The eastern part of the route, from Otley to Wetherby and the villages south of Wakefield, is gently undulating and makes for easy cycling. The western half of the route is hilly, for it breaches the South Pennines. From Denby Dale to Heptonstall and Haworth expect hard climbs.

A functional leaflet describes the route. This is available at tourist information centres in West Yorkshire. The route provides a useful introduction to splendid Pennine villages and amazingly avoids much of the heavy traffic of West Yorkshire.

Mountain Biking

Riders seeking off-road challenge will find some excellent routes in the Peak District. Most of these are set out in two books by Clive Smith titled "Off-Beat Cycling and Mountain Biking in the Peak District" and published by Sigma Press. They illustrate well researched routes prepared by Clive who knows the patch well as a part time ranger for the National Park.

Others might head for the South Pennines. Several routes have been developed by Calderdale Council and publicised in a series of leaflets "Mountain Bike Trails". One, for example, features the Upper Calderdale Valley with rides out of Hebden Bridge and Mytholmroyd, both of which have daily access by rail from Manchester and Rochdale. The routes refer mainly to an excellent network of bridleways, but please ride with consideration for others and take care on the steeper descents.

Traffic Free Rides

Listed below are eight off-road rides which are ideal for people who are keen to cycle away from traffic. These locations are selected because most of them can be reached by train or bus every day of the week from Manchester. Furthermore, several have cycle hire facilities available throughout the year, sometimes at weekend during the winter.

You might also like to take a look at the section below which features cycling opportunities in the Peak District. The Peak District Trails have become justifiably popular and offer a great day out at any time of the year.

Eight Great Traffic Free Outings

	Bus	Train	Cycle Hire	Mileage
Delamere Forest		•	•	15-20 mls
Douglas Valley, Wigan		•		22 mls
Longdendale		•		13 mls
Manifold Valley	•		•	16 mls
Medlock Valley Way	•			18 mls
Middlewood Way	•	•	•	22 mls
Rivington	•	•	•	12 mls
Tatton Park	•	•	•	5 mls

Delamere Forest

Access: Delamere has a daily service from Manchester, except Sundays when trains leave from Altrincham.

Cycle Hire: The Groundwork Trust provides cycle hire from the Discovery Centre at Delamere Forest. It is open daily in July and August and at weekends from Easter to the end of October.

Forest Enterprise has opened up several miles of forestry tracks for use by cyclists and walkers. The routes are traffic free and with very few gradients so Delamere is ideal territory for families. The forest is a mix of deciduous woodland and coniferous and the visitor centre has many interesting displays but do not expect spectacular views from the route. A leaflet and map are available for a small charge.

Douglas Valley

Access: There is a daily train service to Wigan Wallgate, Burscough and intermediate stations with access to the Leeds and Liverpool Canal at Wigan Pier or other bridges.

Cycle Hire: None

When British Waterways assessed its tow-paths for suitability for cyclists, many had hoped for more access. Sadly, this has not been the case. There's a considerable way to go before much of the canal network could be made suitable for cycling. On the sections opened up, you share limited space with the rambler, angler and boater.

One of the loveliest sections to open in recent years is the tow-path of the Leeds and Liverpool Canal which runs through the wooded Douglas Valley between Wigan and Burscough (approximately 11 miles). You can extend your trip by a two-mile ride to Martin Mere Wildfowl Reserve.

Longdendale Trail

Access: Hadfield enjoys a good train service from Manchester on Mondays to Saturdays but unfortunately there is no Sunday service.

Cycle Hire: None

This is a $6\frac{1}{2}$ mile section of the Trans Pennine Trail running through Longdendale. The route has been funded by several organisations, and in many respects is one of the best cycle paths in the country. The ride follows the old Woodhead Valley Railway line from Hadfield Railway Station to Woodhead Station platforms just before the Woodhead Tunnel.

The Longdendale Trail rises slowly and gently up the valley and above the impressive string of reservoirs-Bottoms, Valehouse, Rhodeswood and Torside to eventually come alongside Woodhead Reservoir in promenade fashion. There is a decidedly high level feel about the ride which crosses the Pennine Way and, in the future, the proposed Pennine Bridleway. It offers a promise of the hills without excruciating climbs.

Horse riders are offered a separate pathway along most sections but here they share a path with walkers. There is currently no cycle hire hereabouts and, though there is a visitor centre, there are no places for refreshment except in Hadfield and Padfield. The route is currently worth the journey but in the next few years it will be possible to ride out directly from Stockport to Longdendale, making an ideal long day or weekend break.

The Manifold Trail in The Staffordshire Moorlands

Access: By way of Waterhouses at the southern end of the route on the A523 road between Leek and Ashbourne. GM Buses South, service 201, runs daily from Manchester, Stockport and Water-houses so public transport access is good.

Cycle Hire: There are two centres, Brown End Farm – (01538) 308313 – and at the old Waterhouses Railway Station.

This has to be one of the best cycle paths in the country as the views are spectacular. There are picturesque tearooms at Sparrowlee and Wetton Mill, and a fascinating set of displays at the old railway station terminus of Hulme End.

That's the very joy of the route. It follows the track-bed, now surfaced, of the Leek and Manifold Light Railway. This was a curious affair, built as 2 ft 6 inch gauge, from Hulme End to Waterhouses in 1904. The remainder of the line was standard gauge, i.e. 4 ft 8 inches! As with many such railways aspirations were grand but the light railway did not extend to Hartington or beyond and by the 1930s was seriously in debt. It closed in 1934 and amazingly was opened up as a recreational way a few years later.

You cannot fail to be impressed as the route climbs steadily up the gorge to Wetton Mill. Thor's Cave and the disappearing Manifold river are two of the many interesting sights which cyclists look for, but the entire eight-mile ride is packed with interest. Be warned. It can get incredibly busy on summer weekends. Also note that the section near Wetton Mill and through Ecton Tunnel is shared with cars! This ride along with several others in the Staffordshire Moorlands is part of a 'Cycle and See' promotion – phone Leek T.I.C. for details on (01538) 381000.

Medlock Valley Mountain Bike Route

Access: Daisy Nook Country Park Visitor Centre. There is a bus service to Lumb Lane from Ashton-under-Lyme.

Cycle Hire: None

This 18-mile circular ride follows bridleways mainly, but also some back lanes. It crosses several main roads so it is not entirely traffic free. However, it is possible to follow it up to Hartshead Pike and Bishop Park near Delph, returning by way of Strines Dale and Park Bridge.

The route is way-marked with a horseshoe but it is best to pick up the leaflet which contains instructions. These are not detailed but with a map you can navigate the route where way-marks have gone missing. The route is exhilarating in places and offers a challenge for those who seek a difficult ride with a climb or two.

Middlewood Way

Access: By train to Marple Rose Hill (except Sundays), Middlewood or Macclesfield-daily.

Cycle Hire: At the Groundwork Discovery Centre, Bollington at weekends from Easter to the end of October and daily during July and August. Tel: (01625) 572681.

Another excellent cycle path, using the Macclesfield to Marple disused railway. For most of the route cyclists, walkers and horse-riders are segregated, though cyclists can use the rougher horse route and walkers can share the firmer cycle section. In places there are thin strips of concrete and they are deteriorating now.

The route is great for families. There is always something happening – a pond dip, wildlife safari or other adventures. Nature has been given gentle support in re-establishing herself along the old embankments too. It is traffic free and with very few breaks. The Macclesfield end is metalled and offers a clear run into a major supermarket! From there to the railway station is way-marked but involves crossing highways and riding along short sections of road.

Another enjoyable feature is the easy access to pubs and cafes along the route at Poynton, Wood Lanes and Bollington. There are good views across to Alderley Edge and to Kerridge Ridge where White Nancy is a distinct and much loved local landmark.

While Lyme Park is nearby (and cycling is permitted in the park) it is difficult to get from the Middlewood Way to Lyme. Some like the idea of cycling along the Way and returning along the Macclesfield Canal but please note that cycling is not permitted along the latter. The Middlewood Way has to be on your list for an outing. The only drawback is that on Sundays it is on everyone else's too!

Rivington

Access: By bus from Bolton to Horwich

Cycle Hire: Cycle hire is available at Horwich from D Tours, 49 Hope St, Horwich throughout the year. Tel: (01304) 699460. Roy Hunt offers cycle hire from Lever Park during the summer.

Lever Park is truncated by wide avenues, many of which are designated bridleways and provide the basis for easy rides from the Visitor Centre, where information and refreshment are available.

North West Water have prepared and sell (at a small charge) two rides: an easy one around the reservoirs, which forms the basis of one of the rides in this book; the other is a harder route up the hillside to Rivington Pike. Together they provide 12 miles of good riding but you do need the leaflets as neither is way-marked.

Cycling has become increasingly popular at Rivington. This is not surprising, given the dearth of off-road facilities around North Manchester and the great scenery to be admired here. You might be tempted to call into Rivington Village, a charming group of buildings nestled around the parish church and of course, with a tearoom nearby. The Lancashire Cycleway passes by, but the ride is hard here.

Tatton Park

Access: Train to Knutsford. Ride through the town to the Knutsford Gate.

Cycle Hire: The Groundwork Trust offers cycle hire at Tatton. Tel: (01625) 572681.

In recent years, Tatton Park has encouraged visitors to explore the park by cycle using the road system which runs from the Knutsford to Rostherne Gates. It is possible to ride up to the Old Hall, or the Mere, and other quieter corners from the main car park.

The minor quibble is that some people still drive through the park and there are a few that speed. Most car drivers here, however, are considerate. You also need to be cognisant of people strolling along the lanes. Nevertheless, cycling at Tatton is good fun.

Cycling in The Peak District

This has always been something of a ritual for people from Manchester. It has been the favourite haunt of many cycling groups throughout the decades and has since become a focal point for those who seek off-road trails. Here is a summary of the main routes available:

Carsington Water

Access: There is a special bus service from Wirksworth on summer Sundays in July and August, when the traffic gets really bad; otherwise, a bus runs between Ashbourne and Matlock daily except for winter Sundays.

Cycling around Carsington Water

Cycle Hire: Cycle hire is available daily during the summer and at weekends in the winter. Tel: (01629) 540478.

Lying just off the B5035 road between Wirksworth and Ashbourne, Carsington Water is a showpiece reservoir. It has been designed to cater for the needs of recreationists as well as simply to store water for the Severn Trent Water Company. Part of the complex is devoted to hiring out canoes and water sports equipment and here you will find cycle hire too.

A route has been set out around the reservoir which is where most people ride. The route is a mix of off-road path, back lanes and the B road; now that there are more cyclists on the road, it is much safer than one would expect. The adventurous might escape down the back lanes to Kirk Ireton, Hognaston and Brassington, which have marvellous pubs and fewer visitors than most villages in these parts.

Derwent (Fairholmes)

Access: The A57 road from Glossop to Sheffield cuts through the Upper Derwent Dams and this gets really busy. There's a summer

Sunday only bus 395 which runs directly from Manchester to Fairholmes.

Cycle Hire: Cycle hire is available daily during the summer (weekends only in the depths of winter) from the Visitor Centre where refreshments are also available. 'Phone (01433) 651261 for details.

The Derwent Dams in the Upper Derwent valley are justifiably popular, for the waters are beautiful. The reservoirs achieved fame in 1943 when the 617 Squadron, the Dambusters, practised here. In terms of visitor numbers, Derwent has never looked back. The Peak National Park has been grappling with the influx over the years but it is getting busier, despite all attempts to calm the traffic. The secret is to choose your time to visit. Try earlier in the morning than the crowd and preferably in the week.

Most people cycle along the road which skirts the western banks of Derwent and Howden Reservoirs, for traffic is not welcomed on this road and is restricted almost entirely at weekends. This is easy going, a reasonable climb beneath the dappled shade of the conifers to Upper Clough, where the road ends. Off-road riding begins here and you can circle the reservoir on bridle paths back to Fairholmes. This is less easy than the metalled surface on the western flanks, but is no less enjoyable. This amounts to approximately 10-12 miles cycling in glorious countryside.

There are other bridle routes enabling you to cycle around and above some of the other reservoirs so that you can make a day of it. A mountain bike is absolutely necessary, the climbs are hard and the views are brilliant.

High Peak Trail

Access: Parsley Hay is served by buses on Mondays to Saturdays from Buxton and on summer Sundays only. The southern terminus, High Peak Junction is served by buses from Manchester (Trent R1) daily.

Cycle Hire: Middleton Top (01629) 823204 and Parsley Hay (01298)

84493 Open most days throughout the year but check before travelling in winter months.

This is an excellent route using the track-bed of the Cromford and High Peak Railway. The intention was to build a canal to link the Peak Forest and Cromford navigations. This was abandoned in favour of a railway in the late 1820s, a magnificent achievement given the terrain and gradients. The railway ran from the trans-shipment wharf at Whaley Bridge to High Peak Junction workshops until the last section to Parsley Hay was closed in the late 1960s.

Approximately 18 miles of route is available now as a cycle route. Most people aim for the middle section between Parsley Hay and Middleton Top as it is relatively level. The views across the drystone walls, which characterise the White Peak landscape, are superb. However, the quietest section extends northeast towards Buxton from Parsley Hay to Sparklow where a pub greets your arrival. Others cycle south west to High Peak Junction itself but expect steeper climbs and descents as the inclines on this railway were harsh.

A scenic view from the High Peak Trail

Of all of the Peak District routes this one has to be the busiest. The Tissington Trail joins near Parsley Hay, providing additional opportunities. There are several access/exit points where you can ride off to one of the local villages such as Monyash or Parwich.

Monsal Trail

Access: Bakewell Railway Station is the easiest access point to the Monsal Trail which is primarily a walking route. The section from Coombs Road viaduct, on an old road to Rowsley, to Thornbridge Hall near Great Longstone is open to cyclists too, providing a five-mile run each way.

Cycle Hire: Noton Barn Farm near Bakewell. Tel: (01629)

The Monsal Trail follows, approximately, the old Midland Railway main line from Manchester to London, which ran through the Peak District. Plans are afoot to re-open sections of the line so, in the long term, its days as a cycle and walking route are numbered. Meanwhile, this track-bed offers a traffic-free exit to a group of villages including Wardlow and the Longstones. Each has its own charm and levels of traffic are low and even Monsal Head is bearable.

Sett Valley Trail

Access: New Mills (Central) enjoys a daily rail service from Manchester and Hayfield has a daily bus service from Stockport.

Cycle Hire: Cycle hire is available at Hayfield Information Centre at weekends between April and October and daily during the main summer holidays. Tel: (01663) 746222

The nearest route to Manchester, a relatively short cycle path (only three miles each way) which has proved itself over the years as a favourite for families. Access, via the Heritage centre at New Mills and the intriguing gorge known as The Torrs, requires wheeling your bike up and down steps to a point beyond a medical centre. A route is described in Ride 12.

This is ideal for those who want to escape the traffic and enjoy a walk about Hayfield where there are cafes, pubs and shops. Be careful at the intersections with roads.

Tissington Trail

Access: Access is by way of Ashbourne just off the A523 road or at Parsley Hay on the A515 road. Ashbourne enjoys a daily bus service from Manchester and Stockport, Greater Manchester South Bus 201 to Derby.

Cycle Hire: Cycle hire is available at Mapleton Lane, daily during the summer and at weekends in the summer. Tel: (01335) 343156. Parsley Hay – see High Peak Trail details.

Another gem of a route which meets the High Peak Trail near to Parsley Hay is known as the Tissington Trail. It passes through the idyllic estate village where the first well dressing of the year takes place.

The 13-mile route to Parsley Hay is best approached from the Ashbourne End as the climb up to Parsley Hay is tackled when you are at your freshest and the gentle descent later in the day comes as a welcome bonus. You can divert from Mapleton to Blore and Ilam, and back to the trail at Thorpe, via back lanes but choose early or late in the day when the traffic has subsided.

Longdendale and Manifold Trails

For a description of the Longendale and Manifold Trails see the Chapter on Traffic Free Rides. These routes are excellent and are so easy to achieve by public transport from Manchester.

Ride 1: Barrow Bridge

A ride to the moors above Bolton through one of the model industrial villages of the past and returning through pleasant farming country.

Start: Moss Bank Park on the A58

Distance: 12 miles

Map: O.S. Landranger 109 Manchester

Terrain: Moderate to Hard Going. Mountain Bike or hybrid preferred as there are several off-road sections on difficult surfaces

Level of Traffic: There a few busy sections and crossings

Rail access: Not applicable

Refreshment: Several hostelries on route

Places of Interest:

Barrow Bridge

This is probably one of the best examples of a compact model industrial village scarcely touched by 20th century development. The village was created by Robert Gardener who acquired the Dean Mills Estate north of Bolton. He teamed up with industrialist Thomas Bazley to build cotton spinning and doubling mills, housing for the work-force, a co-operative shop and an Institute for education and social gatherings.

Both Bazley and Gardener were devout humanitarians and tee-totallers so there are no pubs in the village. Nor are there churches, a reflection on their will not to impose sectarian religion on the residents. Barrow Bridge attracted considerable interest among more enlightened politicians and writers of the time, including Disraeli. In his book, he is thought to have partly based his description of Millbank on Barrow Bridge. Part of the valley is now a conservation area.

Barrow Bridge

Moss Bank Park

These are popular gardens where there is a small 'animal world' and a children's play area.

Smithills Hall

A little detour can be made to Smithills Hall, a handsome half-timbered dwelling which is now a museum. Developed by the Ainsworth family, who owned a large bleachworks on the Dean Brook, the present building augments the Great Hall, dating from the 14th century. The rooms reflect different styles from Tudor through to Victorian periods, but most appealing are the impressive timbers exposed throughout the hall.

Wallsuches

Bolton was well known for textile bleaching, and this was one of the earliest centres, making good use of the supply of soft water running off the moorlands. Several of the old works still exist.

The Route

1. From Moss Bank Park turn left to ride along Moss Lane which becomes Barrow Bridge Road. This rises by cottages to cross a little bridge over the Dean Brook. Climb up this narrow lane to a junction with Scout Road.

2. Go left and ride along this splendid moorland road, which dips down to a dell and climbs again. Look for stone cottages on the right known as Dakin.

3. Turn right here onto a narrow lane, which climbs up to a summit. Descend steeply to a sharp right-hand bend, so keep a steady hand on the brake. Keep right at the junction.

4. This road runs through a group of houses at Montcliffe. At the crossroads, bear left to descend by a reservoir. Just beyond, turn left before a bungalow. The lane deteriorates to a track. It is designated as a footpath, so wheel your bike along this section. At the next junction bear left and then climb up through the yard of the works, keeping to the right at the fork. The lane passes by cottages to rise to the main B6226 road.

5. Dismount to cross the road by the public house and go right down Newchapel Lane. This descends to a junction in a housing estate. Turn left and follow this around to Laburnum Grove. Just after the bus stop there is a little link path (dismount here) to Salisbury Road. Go right to the main road.

6. Cycle along for a short section go left up Old Hall Lane. This runs past a hospital and then becomes a rougher track. Pass a farm on the left and continue along a very bumpy surface. This improves as the route progresses through a golf course.

7. At the B6402 go left, but take the next right along another link road passing by the entrance to a farm on the right. The track gives out at modern housing by a large roundabout. Walk left to join the B6226. The road rises towards Horwich and you will soon see The Sportsman's Arms on the left.

8. Dismount to cross the road. Go right to ride along Monserrat Road. Pass a Roman Catholic church and pub and then go along what seem to be carriageways at different levels!

9. Bear left to run down a narrow road through the old quarter and then turn right into Barrow Bridge Road to return to Moss Bank.

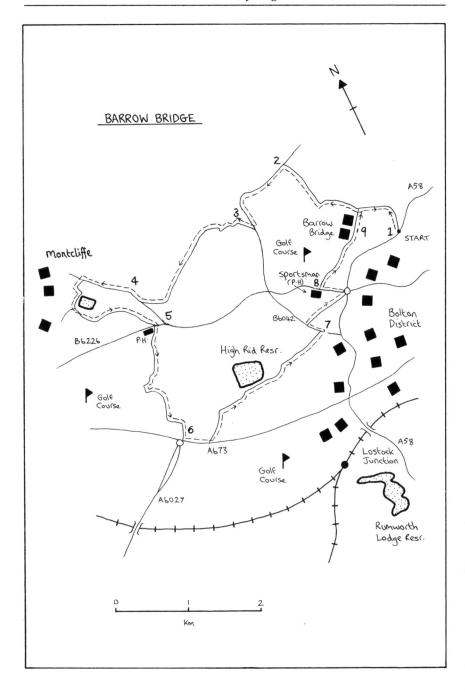

BARROW BRIDGE

Ride 2: Bury

*An outing by steam train and cycle in a part of the world which
has become increasingly popular in recent times.*

Start: Summerseat Railway Station. Please note that this ride involves catching the
train to Summerseat and returning to Bury by bike. Trains usually run at weekends
and Bank Holidays only.

Distance: 5 miles

Map: O.S. Landranger Sheet 109 Manchester

Terrain: A climb out of the Irwell valley but then it is downhill for most of the journey
into Bury.

Level of Traffic: B6214 is busy but otherwise the route is quiet.

Rail access: East Lancs Railway from Bury to Summerseat. Tel: (0161) 764 7790

Refreshment: Bury and Summerseat

Places of Interest:

Bury

It is hard to imagine Bury as a fortified settlement but, in medieval
times, a castle and surrounding earthworks stood high above the
Irwell. By all accounts some of the stonework from the castle was
put to good use in the building of the parish church. According to
historians it seems that Bury was in something of a sorry state during
these early centuries. However, the rise in trade from the growth of
textile production stimulated the local economy.

Bury was home to John Kay, who invented the flying shuttle.
When adopted by manufacturers, it improved weaving substan-
tially, though Kay gained little wealth from his invention. Another
Bury man was Robert Peel, one of the 19th century's greatest
politicians, and a fine memorial to him stands by the church.

Bury's Museum and Art Gallery, only a minute from Bolton Street
Railway Station, houses several famous paintings including some
by Constable, Landseer and Turner. The museum contains several
good reconstructions of early Victorian premises too.

Bury is not an ideal centre to cycle around, as there's far too much traffic, but there's a thriving outdoor market where you can find that much-publicised speciality, the Bury Black Pudding.

Summerseat
This one-time mill village has fast become a desirable area. It includes the superbly restored Brookbottoms Mill, a building which dates from the 1870s, though there were mills on the site prior to this. The cottages in the vicinity were built to house workers at the mill. The setting looks so tranquil now and Summerseat is a favourite spot for those walking the Irwell Valley Way. The Brookbottom railway viaduct was used in filming the television series "Brass".

East Lancashire Railway
Opened with true Victorian pride in 1846, the East Lancashire Railway ran through Radcliffe and Bury to Rawtenstall. It continued as a passenger line until 1972, when it was closed by British Railways. Thanks to the East Lancashire Preservation Society and committed local councils, the line has since been developed as a rural leisure railway with a recent extension to Heywood.

The Route

1. From Summerseat Railway station go left along a track to the village of Summerseat. The track bears right to join a road. Go left to pass the pub and ride over the tight bridge spanning the River Irwell.

2. At the next junction bear left. This runs in a semi-circle back to the railway. Just before the underbridge, go right into Wood Lane. This is a narrow road at first but gives out at a farm to become an unsurfaced track. Climb up to the B6214.

3. After the shops, look for a turning on the left – Hunstanton Drive. This descends through housing to join Woodhill Road on the right. Pass a pub on the left and you soon reach the truncated spurs of an old railway beyond Bainbridge Engineering.

4. Go left to climb the embankment and ride across the bridge. Take the track down on the right to the mill, and ride ahead, along Gordon Road, to Castlecroft Road. This rises up to Bolton Street. Go left for the railway station.

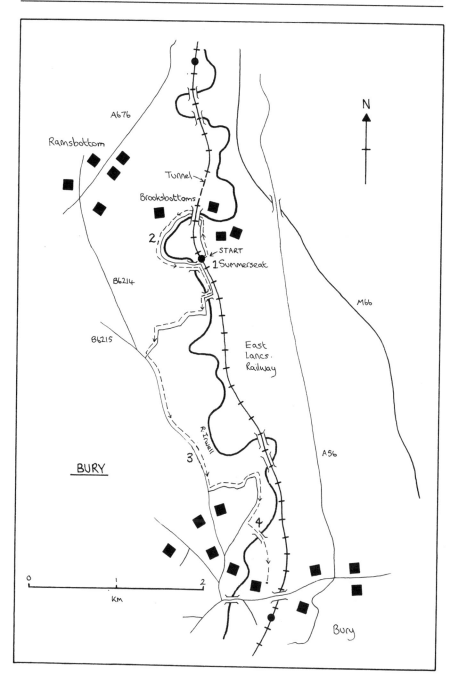

Ride 3: Chelford

An easy ride mainly on back lanes with limited traffic, passing through some of the loveliest countryside in Mid Cheshire.

Start: Chelford Railway Station

Distance: 15 miles

Terrain: Gently undulating plain of Cheshire with no real climbs.

Level of Traffic: Low on all roads except the main A537 at Chelford and a short section of the A50.

Rail access: Direct daily service from Manchester to Chelford and Goostrey for those who wish to cut their ride short.

Refreshment: Several pubs on route and shops in both Chelford and Goostrey.

Jodrell Bank

Places of Interest:

Jodrell Bank

The main radio telescope, admired from miles around, is the second largest in the world. Measuring some 250 feet in diameter, the radio bowl is the same size as the dome of St Paul's cathedral. It monitors radio waves from out in the universe every second of the day.

Jodrell Bank also includes a planetarium, scientific exhibitions of the hands-on variety and a 35-acre arboretum for those who would prefer to be outdoors. As a visitor attraction it is virtually unique.

Peover Hall

Peover stands majestically amid gentle parkland near to a group of hamlets bearing the same name. This was the family home of the Mainwarings for several centuries and the present hall dates mainly from Elizabethan times. Take the opportunity to admire the gables and mullioned windows bedded in a rich red brickwork.

The coach house and stables are also of historic interest but the charm lies with the parish church which has, to all intents and purposes, been a chapel of ease for the Mainwaring family. The church was extensively re-built in the early 1800s but retains many memorials to previous lords and ladies.

The Route

1. From Chelford Railway Station, climb up steps to the pavement. Walk down to the village and cross the road before the Dixon Arms to mount your bike. Ride ahead through the village on this very busy road, but not for long.

2. Go left into Pepper Street, signposted to Snelson. It is about ¼ mile into the hamlet. By the village sign go left into Common Lane and at the fork, keep right. This bends right and runs along to Mill Lane. Go left.

3. Turn first right into Well Bank Lane. This soon bends left and passes the Dog Inn. Ignore the first junction left but at the next T-junction go left. Come to another T-junction and turn right along Grotto Lane. At the crossroads turn left.

4. As the road bends left, go ahead with caution as sight lines are not good. Pass through gates and along an estate road with speed ramps. Despite there being no signs, the estate road is a bridleway, through the parkland of Peover Hall to your right.

5. At the fork bear left unless you wish to visit Peover Parish church. This is now a rougher surface which leads to a bridle-gate by houses.

6. The bridleway now narrows and winds its way gently to a rough track by a market garden. You soon reach the main A51 road. Go left.

7. Pass the Drovers public house and then, at the next junction go left along Booth Bed Lane, a pleasant thoroughfare which bends right and continues for a mile into Goostrey. Go left along Sandy Lane, which deteriorates into a poorly surfaced road. Re-join Main Street and bear left.

8. This seems never-ending as you pass houses and shops. Just before the church, go left.

9. This lane reaches a fork. Bear right for Jodrell Bank. Keep left at the next fork and ahead at the crossroads. The road continues for approximately half a mile and then bends right for Jodrell Bank. It rises above the railway line and then passes by the entrance to Jodrell Bank, which you can hardly miss. Go right if visiting.

10. Proceed ahead to the next junction where you turn left along Bate Mill Lane – appropriate, for it only really serves Bate Mill Farm and one or two other houses, so you should find it exquisitely quiet. There's quite a sharp descent to the old mill and stream. Rise up under the railway arches and to a junction with Grotto Lane.

11. Go right here along Boundary Lane. Follow it through to Mill Lane. Go next right along Chelford Lane to a roundabout on the main A537 road. Then pedal or wheel your bike left up to the railway bridge and Chelford Station.

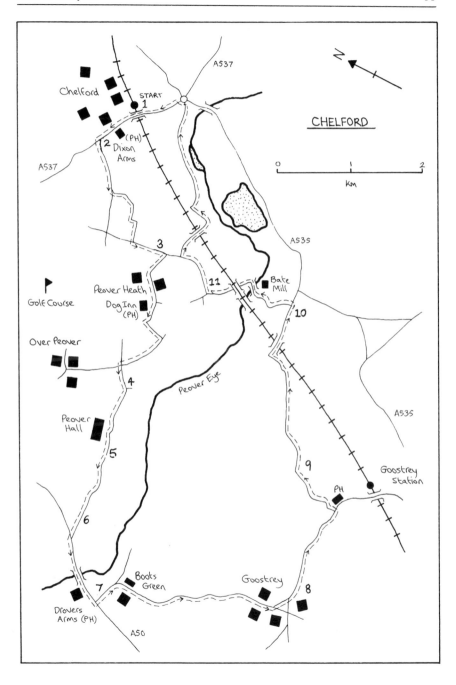

Wigan Pier with Trencherfield Mill in the background

Ride 4: Haigh Hall and Country Park

A mix of moderately busy roads and a cycleway along a disused railway. The ride along the Leeds and Liverpool Canal adds to the variety although this ride can be commenced at Haigh Hall.

Start: Car Park, Trencherfield Mill, Wigan Pier

Distance: 9 miles from Haigh Hall, 21 miles from Wigan

Terrain: Easy going along the canal but the tow-path currently rises to cross several busy roads and there are difficult barriers to negotiate in places. City Challenge investment means that the tow-path is undergoing considerable improvement. Such minor problems do not exist if the ride commences at Haigh Hall but there are two steady climbs on the road route.

Level of Traffic: Beware when crossing the main roads to rejoin tow-paths if starting the route at Wigan Pier.

Rail access: Wigan North Western and Wigan Wallgate stations are near to Wigan Pier but the traffic is appalling here.

Refreshment: Wigan Pier, Haigh Hall and several hostelries on route.

Places of Interest:

Haigh Hall and Country Park

The fortunes of Haigh Hall have been inextricably bound with the extraction of coal, a type known as cannel which burnt with very little smoke. There has been a dwelling on the site since the 14th century but the present hall dates mainly from the 1770s. The then owners, the Earls of Crawford developed mining and ironworks in the estate. The Haigh Foundry made castings for the Laxey Wheel on the Isle of Man and for the first Mersey Tunnel. The hall is now surrounded by an attractive country park.

Wigan

Prior to industrialisation, Wigan was described by that inveterate 17th century traveller, Celia Fiennes, as a "pretty market town". In some respects it has retained that charm but the traffic system makes it very difficult for safe cycle access.

There are fine Victorian buildings to admire and, unusually for this part of the world, Tudor style half-timbered frontages dating from the 1920s – presumably added at the time to raise the appeal of the centre. But, as elsewhere, Wigan's fortunes became inextricably tied to the Lancashire coalfield and the rise of textile production. The working of iron, brass and pewter was also important as were porcelain manufacture and watch-making.

The building of an intricate thread of canal and railways truly opened up the area to rapid industrial exploitation. These networks are now being exploited for leisure purposes. Wigan Borough has a policy to develop routes for cyclists and, during the next decade, facilities for cyclists should be much improved.

Wigan Pier, made famous both by George Orwell's novel and George Formby's music hall banter, is no longer a trans-shipment centre but a major attraction in the area. It is renowned for its outstanding use of interpretation techniques to convey the feeling of what life in industrial Lancashire would have been like at the turn of the last century. The Trencherfield Mill Engine houses the world's largest working mill engine and a machinery hall.

The investment in the waterfront of Wigan is evidenced in the rejuvenation of buildings and clearance of derelict land. The Leeds and Liverpool Canal is now open for cyclists and this provides a great traffic-free route in what is otherwise a very busy traffic congested road system. Please remember that you share this with many people who want to saunter along the tow-path so courtesy counts if we are all to enjoy this magnificent recreational asset.

The Route

Starting from Wigan

1. Wheel your bike to the tow-path at Trencherfield Car Park. Turn left and ride along the promenade to cross Chapel Lane which is very busy. Pass a major junction and wharf before riding under a railway bridge to cross another main road.

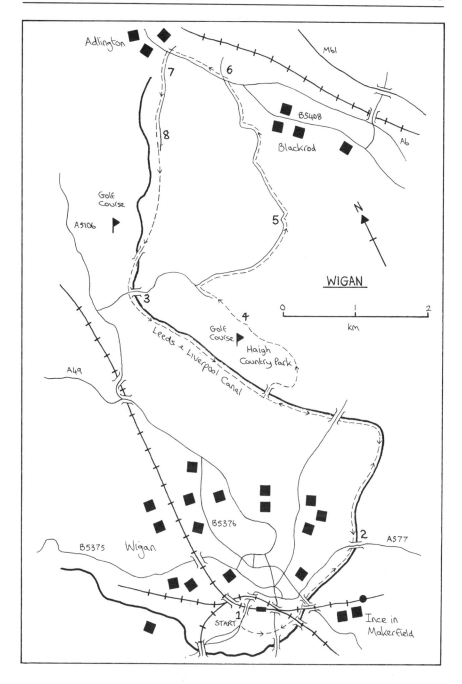

2. Climb the route up the Wigan flight right to the very top where the canal bears left. Continue ahead out into open country. You can see Haigh Country Park to the right.

3. Continue ahead under several bridges, through barriers and finally by moorings to the Crawford Arms. You join a minor road here which exits by the public house at traffic lights onto the B5239. Go right.

Starting from Haigh Hall

4. From the car park at Haigh Hall, go left and follow this road to a junction with the B5239 at Red Rock Lodge about half a mile up from the Crawford Arms. Turn right to climb up the hillside.

5. At the next junction keep left and climb a little more before the road bends before sweeping down to Little Scotland. Climb up once more to a junction where you go left into Dark Lane.

6. Turn left onto the main A6 road, an appallingly busy half mile stretch. You might prefer to wheel your bike along the wide unused pavement on the left. At the outskirts of Adlington, look for the Waggon and Horses pub where a signpost indicates a path left across a green.

7. The path soon reaches a junction by a stream where you bear left and right to join the Red Rock cycle route.

8. Follow this to a car park by the B5239 at Red Rock. Turn left again and, if returning to Wigan, go right at the Crawford Arms; otherwise, ride up to Red Rock Lodge for a right turn again to Haigh Hall.

Ride 5: Heywood

A ride to Cheesden valley and Ashworth Fold, passing through the home ground of Samuel Bamford, writer and philantropist. There are climbs on the route. The ride is partly along bridleways and partly on back lanes. There are a few roads to cross and sections of roads which require care.

Start: Heywood Market Place

Distance: 5 miles

Map: O.S. Landranger 109 Manchester

Terrain: Hilly with two sections of bridleway where surfaces are rough.

Level of Traffic: Busy at road junctions and the first leg out of and the last section to Heywood and but otherwise quiet.

Rail access: None

Refreshment: Heywood and the Egerton Arms

Places of Interest:

Heywood

Standing above the banks of the Roch, the small town of Heywood truly owes its existence to the cotton business. Yew Mill, for example, has always been quoted as one of the largest cotton spinning mills in the world. Needless to say, the town was hit badly during recessionary times and textiles play a lesser role now.

In terms of recreation, there are two new attractions in the area which might be combined with the short cycle ride: one is Chamber House Urban Farm, open all year for people to see the way of life at a mixed working farm; the other is the East Lancashire Railway through to Bury and Rawtenstall.

The Cheesden Valley is much loved by country-goers and is crossed by footpaths, but there is little opportunity for the cyclist to explore this wild area. You will see the beauty of the valley when

Hooley Bridge (leaving School Lane)

dropping down to Hooley Bridge on the return section. You first pass the timeless settlement known as Ashworth Fold, little changed over the years and an indication of what the entire area would have been like prior to industrialisation.

The Route

1. From Heywood Marketplace proceed left along York Street and then follow the main A58 road to the outskirts. Turn left before Ryecroft House into Crimble Lane.

2. This soon descends into the Roch Valley to the mill at Crimble. The road crosses the river and bends left and right by the mill.

3. It then rises as a bridleway up the hillside to join a metalled drive to The Crimble restaurant. Keep ahead to the main Bury Road, opposite the Winston Churchill pub and restaurant.

4. Cross the road and just to the left is Kenyon Fold. Go up here and along a bridle-path on the left to Highlands Road. This leads to the Norden Road by Bamford Chapel.

5. Go right and then next left along a bridleway known as Jowkin

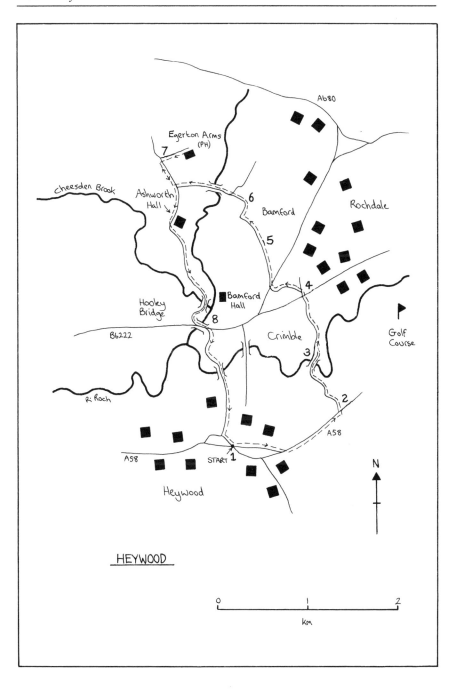

HEYWOOD

Lane. Before Upper Jowkin Farm, go right at the junction and then bear left at the next. This runs by a farm to a narrow road.

6. Turn left to descend rapidly to the valley of the Naden Brook. The climb is equally steep. Rise up along School Lane to a junction beyond the old school. Go right up the hill and next right to the Egerton Arms.

7. After refreshment return to the junction and turn left to descend to Ashworth Fold. The road continues to descend to a mill on the Cheesden Brook. It climbs up to Hooley Bridge.

8. The last section of the ride is less attractive. Cross over (best to dismount) the Bury Old Road and turn right into Bamford Road. Climb back to Heywood.

Ride 6: High Legh

This ride is easy going. It follows a series of level, relatively narrow and lightly trafficked lanes to Arley Hall then runs along wider roads to Great Budworth. There are more cars moving at higher speeds but the sight lines are good.

Start: By the Garden Centre in High Legh

Distance: 17 miles

Map: OS Landrangers 109 Manchester and 108 The Potteries

Terrain: Gently undulating

Level of Traffic: Quiet

Rail access: Not available

Refreshment: Great Budworth

Places of Interest:

Arley Hall and Gardens

The distinctive gardens have been in the caring hands of one family for over 500 years. They include a walled and scented garden and lavish herbaceous borders. The hall was extensively rebuilt in the 1830s by Rowland Egerton-Warburton. There is a charming inscription over the main entrance: "This gate is free to all good men and true. Right welcome though to pass through."

The house is Elizabethan in style and is open to the public at certain times. There is also a private chapel and tithe barn, which add to the considerable character of the estate.

Great Budworth

This is one of the finest estate villages in England and belonging to Arley Hall. The main street, with its half-timbered and red brick houses, are very pleasing to the eye. The sandstone parish church is a good example of perpendicular architecture with some parts dating from the 14th century.

The Route

1. From the junction at High Legh Garden Centre follow Halliwells Lane away from the village, signposted to Pickmere, passing Dairy Farm.

2. At the first junction, turn right along Goldborne Lane. You reach another farm on a corner. Go right at the next junction.

3. Once gain go right at the next junction by a farm. The road curves in a semicircle across the levels of Sink Moss, a pocket of the Netherlands in the North West.

4. Go right at the next junction and ride the short stretch to the wider and busier Swineyard Lane. Turn left and ride over the M6 motorway. After a track on the left and houses on the right, go next left along a road which runs across an old airstrip.

5. The concrete road curves right, then soon bends left to become a narrow lane again. The lane through to Arley is narrow and sometimes winding, so listen out for oncoming traffic.

6. You reach a junction at Sandilands. Go left to follow the lane past a track to Park Farm, then bend right for a final stretch to the crossroads at Arley. Go left for Arley village and hall.

7. After visiting, ride back to the crossroads and turn left. Ride along a tree-lined road to the next junction and turn left. The road bends sharp right at Hollies Farm and wends its way to Greensires Green. Only go right at Keepers Lane if you require the shop and post office at Antrobus. At the end of Keepers Lane go left into the village, with its shop and telephone kiosk.

8. Otherwise, continue to the main road. Turn left. Ignore Pole Lane on the right and the next right. Follow the primary road to a cross roads at Budworth Heath.

9. At the junction, go right into Great Budworth. Ride out of the village on the same road, but do not turn left this time. This section is part of the Cheshire Cycleway.

10. At the next junction, telephone kiosk on the right, go left and keep ahead through Moss End, ignoring the turn to Arley Hall.

11. At Bate Heath, pass by the rose fields of Curbishley Nursery. Go left at the junction after the lay-by and telephone kiosk. This wide lane runs back to High Legh.

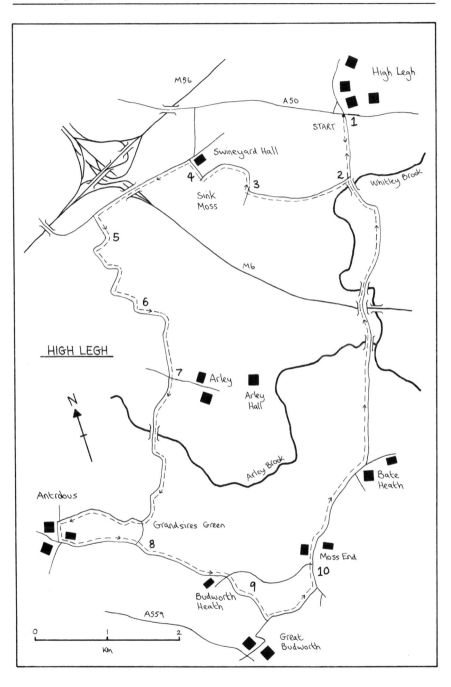

Ride 7: Manchester

Part ride, part stroll as you venture through Manchester's central area. An insight into a city that is fast becoming a place to be. The traffic can be avoided if you choose a Sunday morning for the ride.

Start: Piccadilly Railway Station

Distance: 2 miles

Map: A street map is better in this instance than the Ordnance Survey Landranger sheet.

Terrain: Level but with some steps and walking.

Level of Traffic: Heavy. This ride should only be attempted at quiet times as several junctions are difficult to negotiate and the fumes from cars do not add to the pleasure. Recommended for Sunday morning only!

Rail access: Trains to Manchester Piccadilly

Refreshment: Cafes and pubs on the route

Places of Interest:

Manchester

The Cotton masters brought to Manchester a reputation for innovation and brutal commercial aptitude. Trading links were extensive and the growth of warehouse, mills, canals and railways changed the face of the city beyond recognition during the early 19th century. Such rapid growth in Manchester and the industrial towns of Lancashire also brought massive immigration, abject poverty and social unrest. The latter culminated in the Peterloo Massacre of 1819.

Those eminent Manchester Victorian entrepreneurs also chose to invest in their city. Their legacy is some of the finest edifices in the country, many of which are still functioning today, albeit for other uses. The rejuvenation of this Victorian splendour and the attention given to the restoration of the urban fabric during the past decade is a tribute to those re-shaping Manchester for the post-modern era. Their efforts will be chronicled with equal fervour in years to come.

Walking is a great way to see the city, but it takes a long time. The compromise is to cycle instead. Pick a quiet time such as Sunday morning when the route can be enjoyed relatively safely and without fear of heavy traffic.

The route suggested here does not cover the entire central zone but you can easily add to it. For example, by using the cycle ways on Oxford Road a short detour can be made to the Manchester Museum or the Platt Fields Museum of Costume, both of which rank high in terms of exhibits.

This is a ride which, above all else, celebrates the statues and sculptures that adorn the streets of Manchester. They are very often taken for granted by those who work in the city, but they are an integral part of the much improved central core; they are works of art, accessible to us all. Our Victorian forefathers would be duly proud of their restoration and they would most probably enjoy the recent additions too.

A Manchester tram

Here is a check-list of those you should see on the route and other attractions. They are mentioned in the instructions:

Castlefield Urban Heritage Park

Designated as a park, this heritage area is at the forefront of Manchester's recreation revival. The area is a mix of canals, wharfs, magnificent railway structures, trans-shipment sheds and warehouses. Many of the buildings now serve as hotels, apartments and offices.

Two of the best-known stand side by side. You pass them on the ride. The first is The Museum of Science and Industry, which is on the site of the world's first passenger railway station, Liverpool Road. There are 14 galleries packed with exciting adventures from the discovery of Manchester sewers to space technology. Next door, in Water Street, is Granada Studio Tours, Britain's only serious attempt at a film and TV tour with firm favourites Baker Street (of Sherlock Holmes fame) and the Coronation Street set just around the corner.

You also pass by the reconstructed Roman fortress in Duke Street, which somehow seems incongruous amongst the Victorian industrial heritage. The dimensions of the girders supporting the railway, the wharves and warehouses, and under-arches seemingly in industrial use still, make this a fascinating place to linger.

Bridge Street

On reaching Bridge Street, you will see a sculpture "The Doves of Peace" by Michael Lyons on the left. By leaving your bike on the bridge you can also see along the Irwell a statue of Joseph Brotherton, a famous entrepreneur from Salford.

On the left is the Pump House People's History Museum which houses several displays depicting changes in British society during the past 200 years.

St Ann's Square

Those who make the detour to the shopping quarter of St Ann's Square will chance upon Richard Cobden, whose statue dates from 1867. Cobden was revered for his fight to repeal the Corn Laws, which made the cost of staple food cheaper for working people. There's also a Boer War memorial and you might also admire the glass and ironwork of the Barton Arcade.

Albert Square

The Town Hall is a masterpiece of Gothic Revival architecture. It was built in the 1870s to the design of Alfred Waterhouse who won a competition for the work against well over 130 other firms. The building throughout reflects historic connections with the city from Roman times, but emphasises the importance of cotton.

In front is Albert Square, with a fine row of statues awaiting your personal inspection. Of greatest significance is the memorial to Prince Albert himself which dates from 1867; it was restored in 1894 and again in the late 1970s. Nearby stand statues of James Fraser, a Bishop of Manchester, John Bright of Anti Corn Law reputation, Oliver Heywood the entrepreneur, and William Gladstone the Prime Minister. Each has something to commend it but, before you tire of statues, ride around the corner to St Peter's Square for a taste of more modern work.

St Peter's Square

Not quite in the square are two beautiful pieces of work devoted to peace: "Messengers for Peace" and "Struggle for Peace and Freedom". The cenotaph and St Peter's Church Cross are close by. There's also a building on the right known to all recent Manchester scholars, the Central Library. Across the road is the Midland Hotel and, beyond, the G-Mex Centre in the old Central Railway Station.

Piccadilly

In the large pedestrian area next to the gardens you will find a much abused set of statues devoted to a diverse range of Victorians – James Watt, Queen Victoria, the Duke of Wellington and Robert Peel. They are all of grand proportions and tell great stories. The Wellington statue has been the subject of controversy, for people felt he would be best remembered mounted on a horse rather than in Parliament.

The Route

1. Ride down the main station approach from Piccadilly Railway station to the traffic lights. Go immediately left into London Road along the cycle way.

2. Cross the tram tracks. You can see Piccadilly Undercoft here. On the right is the ornate old fire station and, to the left, offices where the sign reads "Enquiry, Delivery, Shipping, Cartage and Goods Agents Offices". You then come to the next major junction with Fairfield Street. Dismount, cross at the lights and turn left to walk down London Road towards the railway bridge.

3. Go right along Granby Row into UMIST university complex. You will have to dismount at the pedestrian section. Notice the red wire ropes on the left, Axel Wolkenhaus Technology Arch. A few metres to the left under the railway arch is a sculpture of Archimedes. Walk ahead along Granby Row and you will see a jolly sculpture depicting a bottle of Vimto, with an advertising message "Invigorating Vimto, The Ideal Beverage" by Kerry Merrison. The work is in stained oak and reminds us that Mr Nicholls mixed his first batch of Vimto here in 1908 at this very spot.

4. At the barrier go left into Sackville Street then right past the pub into Charles Street. Watch this right turn here for cars cut across you at the junction as the flow is two way.

5. Cross over Princess St and continue ahead to Oxford Road. Pause as you cross the Medlock Bridge, dated 1867, as a glimpse down the river illustrates what life would have been like here a hundred years ago. Pass by the Lass o' Gowrie, with an excellent tiled frontage. Notice the circular plaque, which indicates that this was the site of a pissotiere, retained for posterity and last used 1896.

6. This is an unusual street with the BBC on the left and a host of unusual small companies opposite. Cross over Oxford Road and take a glance on the right to the old Refuge Building, now a hotel.

7. Continue ahead between old mills and warehouses to Cambridge

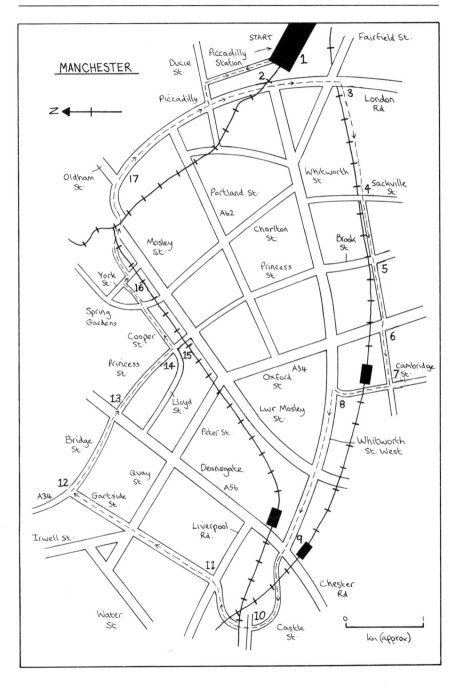

Street, a difficult right turn. This passes the boundary for the city at the river and the famous Hotspur printing works.

8. Go left into Whitworth Street. Note the old pieces of purification machinery on the left between the arches and the modern British Council building. Keep ahead at Medlock Street Junction to Deansgate railway station and Deansgate itself. Note the sculpture of the Penny Farthing to the left.

9. Dismount to cross Deansgate and proceed ahead along Castle Street into Castlefield, currently an area which is being beautifully restored. Castle Street, which has a surface of setts, offers a great view over Castle Quay and bends right to a good pub stop, Dukes 92.

10. Ride over the canal and the road bends right, or you can walk down to the wharf by the Castlefield Hotel if you prefer. The road, known as Duke Street, winds up Liverpool Street. There's an awkward crossing here; if necessary, use the zebra crossing to the left.

11. Proceed ahead along Lower Byrom Street to pass by the Museum of Science and Industry. Cross directly over Quay Street and ride along Gartside Street to Bridge Street.

12. To the left is Albert Bridge and a sculpture by Michael Lyons, "The Doves of Peace". Immediately left is the People's History Museum. Go right into Bridge Street and ride up to cross Deansgate, but be sure to position yourself well in time in the middle lane. Go ahead into John Dalton Street. If you prefer, dismount and cross by foot!

13. Ride up John Dalton Street and look for a small Street on the left known as Ridgefield. Go left here for a detour to St Ann's Square where you can see a statue of Cobden.

14. Otherwise, continue ahead into Albert Square. Dismount at Princess Street by the Town Hall and walk across the pedestrian crossing. When you have taken a close look at the line of statues, go left down Lloyd Street. As it bends left, go right on the cycle way through to St Peters Square. Here, there are more statues in the Peace Garden, "The Messenger of

Peace" by Barbara Pearson, 1986 and the magnificent "Struggle for Peace and Freedom" by Philip Jackson.

15. On the right is the Central Library and ahead the Midland Hotel, otherwise known as the Holiday Inn Crowne Plaza. Retrace your wheels back to Lloyd Street but turn right to the junction across Princess Street. At the end of the corner you can just see the City Art Galleries, which have a superb range of paintings on view.

16. Keep ahead up Fountain Street until you reach York Street. Go right and then left into West Mosley Street. This bends right into Piccadilly Gardens. This is potentially dangerous: there are so many buses and trams turning in all directions that it is best to go left and wheel your bike around right to Piccadilly. Cross over to the central area of the Gardens and turn left to inspect the fine statues of Victorian dignitaries and royalty.

17. Cross over the pedestrian crossing at the far end by the Portland Hotel and walk your bike left up to the crossing over the east end of Piccadilly. Turn right to ride along the cycle way down to the traffic lights and Piccadilly Station approach.

Ride 8: Middlewood

An introduction to the Middlewood Way and the gently undulating landscape of the eastern fringe of Cheshire. There are a few climbs.

Start: Marple Rose Hill Station

Distance: 15 miles (8 miles if joining at Middlewood Station)

Terrain: Easy

Level of Traffic: Moderately busy on back lanes near Higher Poynton

Rail access: Marple Rose Hill or the ride can be started at Middlewood Railway Station

Refreshment: Cafe and pubs at Higher Poynton, Coffee Shop

Places of Interest:

Lyme Park

Lyme Hall is a magnificent mix of Elizabethan, Georgian and Regency styles of architecture. The hall is set in gardens which reach to an extensive wild parkland where there are landmarks such as the Cage (a former hunting tower dating from 1520).

Cycling is permitted along the roads of the Park but unfortunately there is no traffic free link between Lyme Park and the Middlewood Way.

Middlewood Way

The Middlewood Way uses the former railway line between Macclesfield and Marple. Opened in 1985 by David Bellamy it has been a tremendous success. Nature has reinstated herself with a little help from the Rangers. There is a full programme of activities throughout the year, including pond dipping and hedge laying, to allow people close access to this resource.

As with many of the traffic-free routes of the North West, there is considerable demand for cycling, alongside walking and horse-riding. Sunday afternoon can become quite congested.

The Middlewood Way

The Route

1. From Rose Hill Station, turn left and left again along Station Road to join a rough track. This is the start of the Middlewood Way. This runs behind houses and into the countryside. Continue to High Lane where a tunnel takes you beneath the busy A6 road. Continue to Middlewood Station.

2. For those joining at Middlewood Station: push your bike up from the platform to join the Middlewood Way on the overbridge. Go right (unless you have arrived on from the Buxton direction, then it is a left) to ride along the Middlewood Way.

3. Continue until you reach the old railway station platform at Higher Poynton. Then push your bike up the ramp to exit opposite the Boars Head. Next door, there is a cafe, so there's plenty of refreshment on hand.

4. Turn left to ride along Shrigley Road North. At the next junction, go right to glide down Coppice Road towards Poynton. There's more traffic on this road. Pass the Late Shop and turn next left along Waterloo Road.

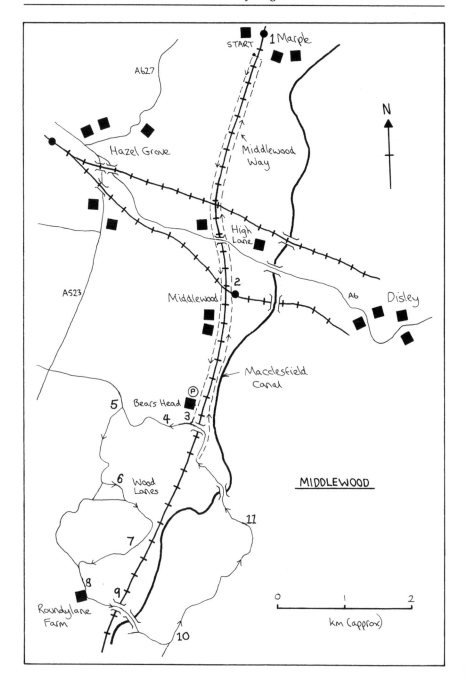

5. The houses are left behind and you soon reach Moggie Lane. Go left to cross the Poynton Brook to rise to Wardsend. There's a turning on the left along a road with setts, signposted as a footpath only.

6. Otherwise, continue to Wood Lane West where you bear left to climb up Wood Lanes. The Miners Arms is to your left and the entrance to the nursery and tearooms. Ahead is the ever popular Ken's Cabin and access back onto the Middlewood Way for those who have had enough road riding.

7. Otherwise, go right along Wood Lane South. This climbs and then dips before rising again to a narrow section at Booth Green. The road crosses a bridge and reaches a triangular junction. Go left.

8. There's more pedalling as you make your way up to Roundy Farm. Those who wish to deviate to Adlington should bear right (but be careful at this turning as the visibility is not good). Roundy Lane runs down to a junction with the Adlington Road. Turn right and follow it down to Adlington Railway Station and the Legh Arms. Fortunately you are protected by lights across the main road. Continue ahead to Adlington Hall which stands on the left.

9. Otherwise, pedal even harder up Springbank to a bridge by Springbank Farm. You can walk your bike down to the Middlewood Way here and go left to return to Middlewood. If not, cycle over the Macclesfield canal and up to a junction.

10. Go left and then left again at the next junction where the Pott Shrigley Hotel is advertised. The road is signposted left to Higher Poynton. This road dips at first but after the Coffee Tavern (a converted chapel) there's something of a climb up Harrop Brow rewarded only by views of South Manchester.

11. Then it is plain riding down to the tunnel beneath the canal, dripping wet and as dark as night so a light definitely improves safety here. The road winds its way down to the car park at Poynton Coppice. At the far end near rejoin the Middlewood Way for the return saunter back to Middlewood Station.

Ride 9: Milnrow

Primarily a hard off-road ride which requires a sturdy mountain bike and a degree of stamina. Great bridleways and excellent scenery.

Start: Milnrow Railway Station

Distance: 6 miles

Map: O.S. Landranger 109 Manchester

Terrain: Moorland bridleways, hard going and should not be attempted in poor weather.

Level of Traffic: Very quiet except for light traffic in Milnrow.

Rail access: Milnrow

Refreshment: There are pubs and cafes in Milnrow and Newhey.

Places of Interest:

Milnrow

Milnrow was a traditional mill town which grew out of a weavers' settlement; some houses retain garrets from the 17th and 18th centuries. One reminder of its former importance in textiles is the Ellenroad Engine House in Newhey (you pass near to it on the return leg). It is thought to be the home of the largest working mill engine in the world. The Engine House is usually open and in steam on the first Sunday of the month.

Milnrow is best known in folklore terms as the home of dialect poet John Collier, writing often under the name of Tim Bobbin. All of his works are available in Rochdale library. For those seeking other cycling routes in the Milnrow, Rochdale and Littleborough area pick up a copy of the booklet "Safer Cycle Routes in and around Rochdale", available for a small charge in the Rochdale area.

South Pennines and Piethorne

This is a route where there are many opportunities to enjoy extensive views across Greater Manchester and across traditional South Pennine scenery.

The reservoirs here were built from the mid 19th century to 1901 to serve the growing demands from industry and local populations in Oldham and Chadderton for improved water supplies. They have been developed in recent years for recreational purposes as well as water storage.

The Route

1. From Milnrow Railway station ride along Station Road to Dale Street. Turn right but look for the third turning left, Charles Street. This is next to Albert Street, so watch for traffic at this awkward turning.

2. Charles Street runs through housing up to a large mill known as Butterworth Hall. Despite gates and notices the bridleway runs to the left of the building and continues along a lesser track to join another to the right of a cottage.

3. Go right at the junction to go under the motorway. Turn left and as the track rises to a fork keep right to pass to the right of Newfield Head Farm.

4. Continue ahead up Carr Lane, a sunken and wet patch of bridleway to a junction. Turn right to ride on a better surface.

5. The bridleway rises up to a bridle-gate. There are good views of the reservoirs to the right. Go through this another gate. The route is well defined, dipping and rising. The climb ahead is in a sunken section and wet. You will see that some people have walked to the right of this section.

6. The bridleway bends right and emerges at a drier spot where it meets another route. Go right here and you will soon find that the route drops between Turf Hill and Binns Pasture to the top of Piethorne reservoir.

7. On the left is the smaller Norman Hill Reservoir. The track runs between tall walls with a nature reserve to the right. Go through the gate. Keeping ahead, cycle up the hillside to a junction where you go right.

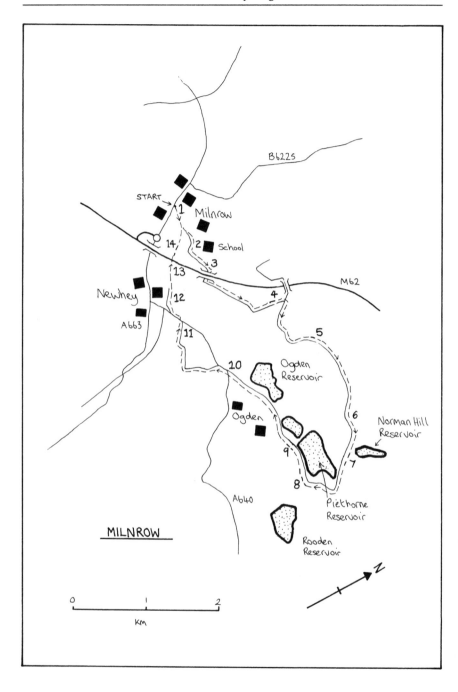

B6225

START

1 Milrow

Milnrow

14

2 School

3

13

M62

Newhey

12

4

A663

11

5

10

Ogden
Reservoir

Ogden

6

Norman Hill
Reservoir

9

7

8

Piethorne
Reservoir

A640

Rooden
Reservoir

MILNROW

0   1   2

Km

N

8. The track runs beneath a small reservoir and then joins the fishermen's path alongside the rippling waters of Piethorne. You will come to a kissing gate and barred gate where you will have to lift your bike over.

9. At the end of the reservoir continue ahead on the metalled road. There's a pleasant run down to Ogden, part of which is now a conservation area. Watch for the speed ramps.

10. Go straight across at the Huddersfield Road into Bethany Lane, a quaint little thoroughfare no more than a carriage width. This winds its way down to Haugh where a cobbled road comes to a junction beyond a pub.

11. Go right along Haugh Lane and at the main road turn left.

12. Before reaching the railway station go right after the pub up a narrow road known as Church Street which leads up to Newhey church.

13. Keep ahead along a track, which soon narrows to the width of a path – so walking might be preferable here. It drops down to a memorial garden before the motorway.

14. At the main road turn right to return to Milnrow.

Ride 10: Mobberley

A ride through the back lanes of Cheshire between the village of Mobberley and Lindow Common in Wilmslow.

Start: Mobberley Railway Station

Distance: 8 miles

Terrain: Easy Going

Level of Traffic: Quiet back lanes and short sections of bridleways. A few sections of busy road.

Rail access: Mobberley Railway Station

Refreshment: Several hostelries on route

Places of Interest:

Mobberley church

Lindow Common

This was once an important source of peat extraction; it continues today on a more modest scale. In 1984, a remarkable discovery was made here of the body of "Lindow Man", thought to be several thousand years old and preserved beyond all expectations in the peat.

Mobberley

A thirteenth century priory once existed here, but the present church dates from mainly the fourteenth and fifteenth centuries. The church has a superbly carved wooden screen and a stained glass window dedicated to Leigh-Mallory who died in 1924 climbing Mount Everest.

The Route

1. From the entrance to Mobberley Railway Station, turn left along Station Road. At the next junction, make a right turn for Mobberley along Hobcroft Lane, which becomes Church Lane. Follow this through to Mobberley passing by the church and the Church Inn.

2. At the main road go left. The road climbs and then levels to run through the village. Go left down Newton Hall Lane before the Bird in Hand public house. There is a bakery opposite.

3. Follow this ahead and at the junction keep left. The lane winds its way past a golf course and to Morley Green along Burleyhurst Lane. As you approach Morley Green, turn right down Eccups Lane, blessed with speed ramps. You know you have past it if you reach the junction in Morley Green.

4. This would bring you to Mossways residential caravan park. Instead, you keep ahead along a narrow path behind the caravans on the right. It is a bridleway and soon widens to a track. Take care as access traffic uses this section.

5. The main track turns left but you keep ahead along a woodland path through Lindow Moss to Lindow Farm and then along Lindow Lane. As you begin to see the road and houses ahead, look for a turning left. This leads up to a road. Go left.

6. You next join Racecourse Road by Lindow Common. Go left and, at the corner behind the Boddington Arms public house, go ahead along a rough road. This brings you to the main A538 road. However, go left again along an unmade road. Follow this ahead.

7. Turn left into Burleyhurst Lane to ride through Morley Green again and to the outskirts of Mobberley.

8. At the first road junction, go right into Davenport Lane. The sight lines are reasonably good but watch out for traffic here. Continue straight on at the next junction, i.e. along Blakeley Lane, but not for long.

9. Turn next left into Ostlers Lane and right into Wood Lane. Follow this around until you reach Small Lane. Go left and then turn right into Station Road – it is an awkward one.

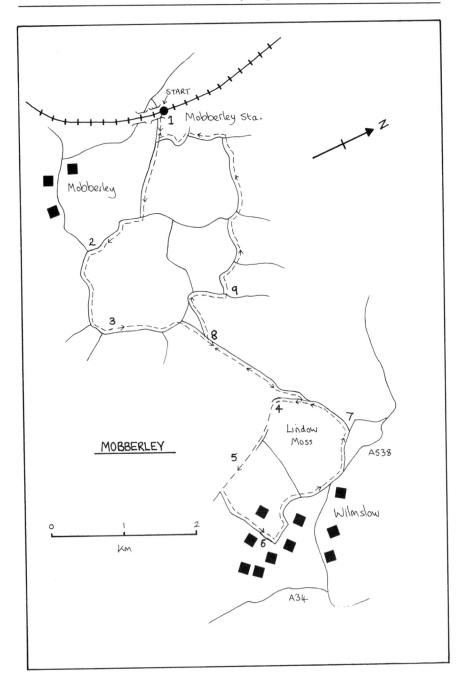

START

1 Mobberley Sta.

Z

Mobberley

2

3

9

8

4

Lindow
Moss

MOBBERLEY

5

A538

7

Wilmslow

0   1   2
km

6

A34

Ride 11: Mossley

The first section of the ride is easy going, being on the old Tame Valley loop railway line. Those seeking to explore Diggle and Delph will need to be able to cope with hillier territory. Either way, this is a good way to explore Saddleworth.

Start: Mossley Railway Station

Distance: 8 miles easy or 12 miles on the extension.

Map: O.S. Landranger sheets 109 Manchester and 110 Sheffield and Huddersfield area

Terrain: Mainly on old railway track-beds – easy going but the extension to Diggle and Dobcross has several climbs.

Level of Traffic: Very quiet except for traffic in Mossley and Uppermill.

Rail access: Mossley.

Refreshment: Several pubs and cafes in Uppermill.

Places of Interest:

Mossley

Prior to local government reform in the 1970s, Mossley had the misfortune of straddling three county boundaries – Cheshire, Lancashire and Yorkshire. This was reflected in there being three MPs, three parish churches, three registry offices, and so on – which was often tedious for the residents.

As with so many communities in the Tame Valley, Mossley's fortunes were tied to the production of woollen goods. This peaked in the early decades of the 19th century and thereafter was superseded by cotton manufacture. There are a few survivals from the time reflecting the wealth brought to owners of the mills. For example, one impressive building is the Italianate style "Whitehall", built first as a dwelling, then used as a town hall and now commercially.

Brownhills Visitor Centre

Situated at the top end of Uppermill the visitor centre stands between the Wool Road and the Huddersfield Canal near to the Woolroad Basin. This was once a trans-shipment centre. The Huddersfield Canal was opened in 1811 and is the highest in Britain. It was admired for its engineering ingenuity at the time, especially the Standedge Tunnel at 3 miles and 409 yards! The canal has been much restored but the tow-paths are not available for cyclists.

The Brownhills Visitor Centre contains several exhibitions illustrating life in the area; it is open daily except Mondays. On the other side is Saddleworth Viaduct, very pleasing to the eye with its lock and skewed arch.

Saddleworth

Saddleworth is the name given to describe the entire area. It encompasses the towns in the valley bottoms as well as the dispersed rural villages and folds nestling in the higher shoulders of the valley. These folds were originally farming communities and many farmers supplemented their living by weaving wool. Not surprising when

Uppermill

you survey the bleak moorland tops. Some of the stone dwellings date from the 17th century. They are characterised by mullioned windows to allow more light in and "tak-in" steps to the first floor work-room to where bales of wool would be delivered, and from where finished goods were despatched.

Greenfield and Uppermill are the main towns. They both expanded rapidly with the growth of the cotton industry during the last century. Many mills survive but they do not serve their original purposes. Uppermill, in particular, has become popular with its craft shops and cafes on every corner. On Sundays, the influx of car-borne visitors overwhelms a community which, until very recently, knew a very different way of life. In the centre is the Saddleworth Museum, which illustrates the ways of old.

Dobcross and Delph have the gone the same way, but less intensively. The Saddleworth Festival is one of the best celebrations of folklore and music in the North West.

Delph was linked to the main railway line by a curious little branch line; in the 1850s, the train was horse-drawn. It was so slow, even after steam appeared, that locals nick-named it the "Delph Donkey". The track-bed forms part of the ride as does the old loop line from Stalybridge to Greenfield

The Route

1. From Mossley Railway station cross the road and ride down the one way Mill Street to Micklehurst Road. Cross the canal bridge and turn second left into Station Road. The entrance to the cycle route is to the left of the restored Micklehurst railway station.

2. Ride the cycle route above the flood plain of the River Tame and the restored canal. It comes to the Huddersfield Road which needs care. Cross over this and the Manchester Road to rejoin the cycle route. The Royal George pub stands to the left of the crossroads.

3. Continue ahead to rise up to the next straight section of the route to Greenfield, where the track reaches the main Chew Valley Road.

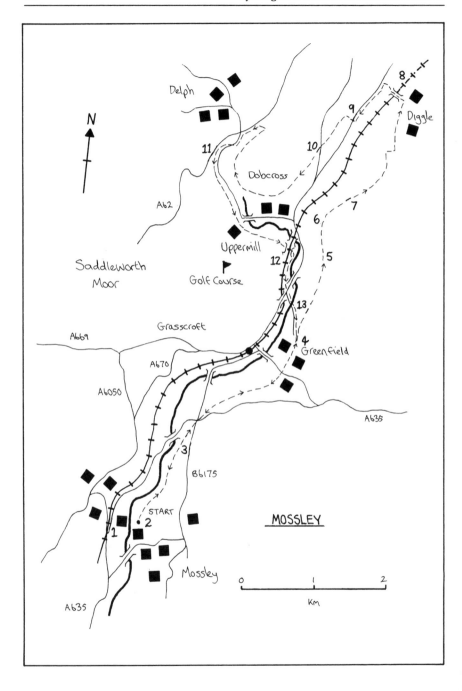

4. The ride now proceeds along the old line to the back of Uppermill. This was squeezed between development and over new bridges to avoid crossings below. It runs by a leisure centre and ahead through open ground.

5. It then crosses a private drive and climbs a steep bank, which curves left to Brownhills Lane.

6. Those wishing to take the short route should go left down to the main road at Brownhills and cross to the Visitor Centre. Then pick up the instructions at Paragraph 12

7. Those looking for a harder ride should bear right at Brownhills Lane. Climb up to fold at Field Top. The lane is now known as Moor Lane and rises up to a junction with High Stile Lane. Go left and then ahead for Diggle, keeping to the right at the triangular junction. This section has several ascents and sharp descents.

8. Arrive in Diggle for a well deserved break. The Diggle Hotel stands ahead and to the right is a dead end to Diglee Fold. Go left here over the canal and railway and left again to follow Sam Road to the Huddersfield Road. Go left again.

9. The turn for Dobcross is just after The Hanging Gate pub. Be aware of traffic when making the right turn at the junction into Spurn Lane. It bends left and climbs up to the A670, which is busy, but the sight lines are good.

10. Once, over ride up Sandy Lane which offers great views across Saddleworth. This descends sharply to the centre of Dobcross by The Swan public house where you bear right into Platt Road. This rises out of the village then descends sharply into Delph opposite Bell House. Go left on the main road and left again at the junction.

11. Pass the terminus of the one-time Delph Donkey; there is no access here at New Delph Road. Approximately a quarter of a mile along this road, opposite an entrance to the Diamond Works, go right into Shutt Lane, a manoeuvre best walked. Ahead is the access to the old track-bed. Join it and bear left to ride to the Brownhills Visitor Centre.

12. Here you join Moorgate Street, which runs beneath the railway viaduct and into Uppermill. Take care for it is a busy right turn. It is better to use the pedestrian crossing. Go right along the High Street but after the museum go left along Bridge Street. This climbs a little, runs through a housing estate and joins the cycle path at the main road in Greenfield.

13. Return to Mossley as on the outward journey.

Ride 12: New Mills

Riding towards the high hills of Derbyshire along an old railway track is a refreshing way to begin the ride. For those who dislike hills, the Sett Valley Trail should be used for the return. The area is essential for lovers of industrial archaeology. Beware: the second section of the ride has several hard climbs and one rough bridle path.

Start: New Mills Railway Station or Torr Valley Visitor Centre car park

Distance: 12 miles

Map: O.S. Landranger sheets 109 Manchester and 110 Sheffield and Huddersfield

Terrain: Easy on the Sett Valley Trail but hard climbs on the return route via Thornsett and Mellor Moor.

Level of Traffic: Traffic free on the Sett Valley Trail, very quiet minor roads and traffic only in New Mills

Rail access: New Mills (Central) daily

Refreshment: New Mills, Hayfield and Brook Bottom

Places of Interest:

Hayfield

The small township of Hayfield is seen almost as the base camp for explorations of Kinder Scout and surrounding high ground. It has a pleasant main street which is quiet and there are cafes and pubs for refreshment. The penalty is the intrusive by-pass which separates the information centre and Sett Valley Trail.

New Mills

New Mills has always been a small shopping centre for the local population, many of whom were previously employed in the mills which grew up around the Goyt and Sett rivers. Below the town is the spectacular gorge known as "The Torrs". What is intriguing about the place is the mix of natural habitat, old mill sites and the old mills.

The history of the town is captured in displays at the Heritage Centre, particularly the development of mills in the late 18th and early 19th centuries. The Centre is situated just by the bus station on Rock Mill Lane, but there is no substitute for locking the bike up and walking down to the Torrs to look for yourself.

Sett Valley Trail

This was at once the New Mills to Hayfield branch line (originally the Hayfield Joint Railway), which opened in 1868. Closed by British Railways 102 years later Derbyshire took the opportunity to secure it for recreational use. Ironically, trains would have brought thousands of excursionists from Manchester on summer Sundays to walk and picnic in the surrounding moors.

Thornsett

Mentioned in the Domesday Book, this old settlement has changed little in comparison to New Mills, but there is still evidence of lime kilns and coal-pits in the locality as well as cotton manufacture.

The Route

1. From the station, ride or push your bike to the centre of New Mills. Go left here into Market Street then right into High Street. The road descends to a junction near the Pineapple Inn and a corner shop. Go right into Dye House Lane, but take care along here as it is narrow. As the road climbs, go left through the wicket gate.

2. Climb up to cross a pedestrian route and then you are away along the Sett Valley Trail. Follow this to Hayfield. There is a road to cross at Thornsett and Birch Vale (where there's a cafe on the left) so treat this section with caution. The trail emerges at the car park in the old station yard. Pass by the visitor centre.

3. Dismount to wheel your bike through the subway and into Market Street in Hayfield by The George Inn. Go left and then left again into Smallhouse Lane. This becomes Thornsett Lane,

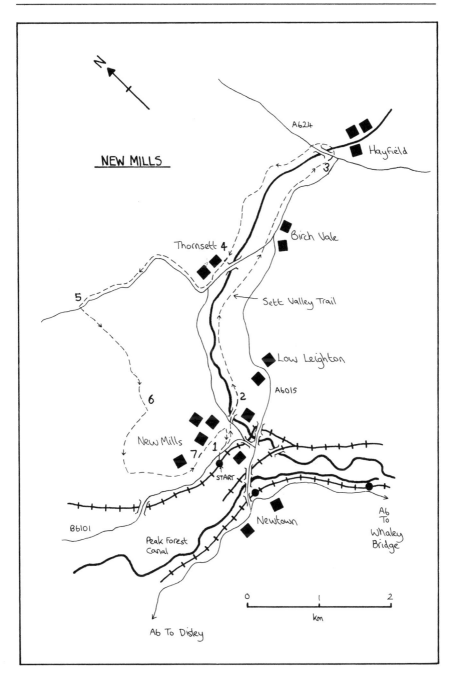

NEW MILLS

N

A624

Hayfield

3

Birch Vale

Thornsett 4

Sett Valley Trail

5

Low Leighton

2

A6015

6

New Mills

7 1

START

B6101

Newtown

Peak Forest
Canal

A6
To
Whaley
Bridge

A6 To Disley

0   1   2

km

which climbs steeply. At the top, prepare for a steep descent to
Thornsett.

4. Turn right by the Congregational church to Mellor along a quiet
    road beneath Thornsett Brows. At the triangular junction, bear
    left and, at Lydiate Farm, begin a long hard climb up to the
    Mellor Road. It is long and hard.

5. Go right then immediately left along an unmetalled road. This
    leads to a junction. Continue ahead.

6. Descend to a junction by a golf course. Go right along an
    unmade road which drops down to Brookbottom. On reaching
    a metalled road turn right for The Strines public house.
    Otherwise turn left for New Mills.

7. Brookbottom Road joins a junction with St Mary's Road. Go right
    here to return to the railway station. Otherwise keep ahead
    until you pass the library and turn right for the town centre

Ride 13: Patricroft

A ride along cycle paths through some of the western suburbs, allowing an opportunity to enjoy traffic-free conditions near to home.

Start: Patricroft Railway Station or Monton Roundabout

Distance: 6 miles

Map: O.S. Landranger sheet 109 Manchester

Terrain: Easy Going

Level of Traffic: Crossing only one major road and a short section of traffic-calmed roads.

Rail access: Patricroft

Refreshment: There are pubs in Patricroft

Places of Interest:

Bridgewater Canal

The early 18th century entrepreneur, the Duke of Bridgewater, made a fortune from the coal deposits beneath his estate. The Bridgewater Canal was the solution to his transport dilemma in that he needed to get his coal from the mines at Worsley to Manchester's industrial heartland. Completed in the 1760s, this was one of the first navigations in the country and this soon followed with an extension to the Mersey running west. Unfortunately bikes are currently banned from the Bridgewater Canal.

Salford Loop Lines

A network of cycle routes is being developed along the old railway lines, known as the Salford Loop lines, which once linked the industries of Salford with main routes.

The Route

1.   From Patricroft Station go right along Green Lane. Before

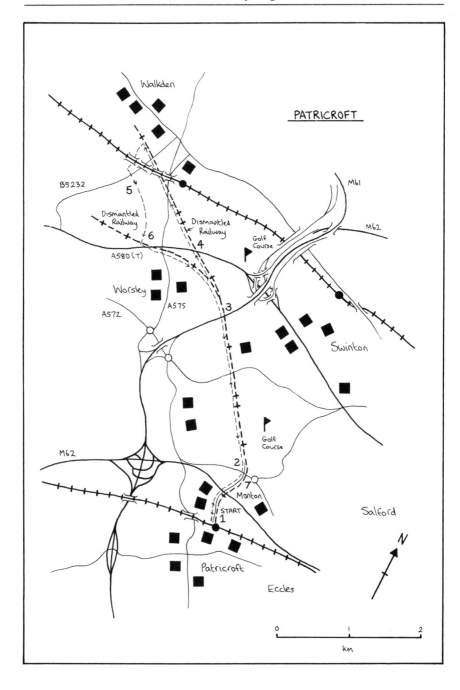

Walkden

PATRICROFT

BS232

5

Dismantled
Railway

Dismantled
Railway

6

4

Golf
Course

A580(T)

M61

M62

Worsley

A575

A572

3

Swinton

M62

Golf
Course

2

7

Monton

START

1

Salford

Patricroft

Eccles

N

0　　　　　　1　　　　　　2

km

reaching the roundabout keep ahead as the main road sweeps right. This is a cul-de-sac. Dismount to cross the road.

2. Those starting at Monton will join here. Go left by the toilets to climb the embankment and your ride begins in earnest, a high level track above the surrounding playing fields. Pass by Worsley Old Station.

3. Ride beneath the M62 road and come to a junction. Ignore the left junction. This is the way you will return. Continue ahead on the Roe Green Loopline. Ride under the East Lancs Road and proceed along the route towards Little Hulton.

4. Unfortunately, the ride gets progressively worse as you make your way towards Little Hulton with litter, detritus and broken glass marring what otherwise would be a superb facility.

5. You approach steps leading up to Parsonage Road. Go left just before the steps along a path below a railway line. Dismount to drop down to Hilton Road. Go left and cross a mini roundabout into Park Road. Then bear next right into Broadway.

6. Follow this traffic-calmed road to the end, where you bear left along a track to join the Tyldesley Loopline. This leads back to the junction where you bear right to return to Monton.

7. At Monton, retrace your route back to Patricroft railway station.

Ride 14: Pennington Flash

*An easy route along a new section of bridleway and on one of the
very few cycle paths alongside main roads in the area. The roads
around Culcheth are quiet mainly but they get busier late
afternoon. The views across arable farming and mosses give a
different feel to the ride.*

Start: Pennington Flash Country Park

Distance: 15 miles

Terrain: Easy Going

Level of Traffic: The road junction at Lane Ends is busy otherwise the roads to
Culcheth and Croft are light to moderately trafficked, depending on the time of day.
The selection of a clockwise direction ride through Culcheth and Croft is safer then
anti-clockwise on this occasion, but watch the right-hand turns!

Rail access: Nearest station is Leigh

Refreshment: Pennington Flash and hostelries on route

Places of Interest:

Pennington Flash Country Park

Coal mining in these parts dates from late medieval times, but it was
only in the last century that mining and textile manufacture changed
the nature of this old established Lancashire market town. The
father of factory production, Richard Arkwright was married in the
parish church of Leigh in 1761.

Pennington Flash exists because of the subsidence caused by past
mining activities, but is now a country park of increasing beauty as
it matures. The range of wildfowl is an attraction in its own right.
The area was served by railways, which superseded the Leeds and
Liverpool Canal in transporting coal and other commodities. In 1831
the Kenyon and Leigh Junction Railway ran by Pennington and part
of this route has been given over to a new road. The bridleway built

alongside shows how easy this can be done and for a very small cost in comparison to all other road building expenditure.

Pennington Flash Country Park

The Route

1. From the main car park by the Visitor Centre ride down the access road, with speed humps, to the main A572 road. Cross over by the Robin Hood pub and walk left by the Fire Station to join a small bridleway. This runs to the right of the road and bears right again.

2. Ride along this nicely landscaped route until it reaches the A580 East Lancs road. The track is at low level, but you have to go up the embankment to join a cycleway along the main road. This is fine except for the lay-bys, where inconsiderate people smash glass and drop litter.

3. This brings you to a side road by houses and then the main A572 again at Lane End, by one of the busiest junctions in the world. Go left and next left into the B5207, Kenyon Lane, towards Culcheth.

4. Stay on this road until you reach Culcheth. Prime yourself for a

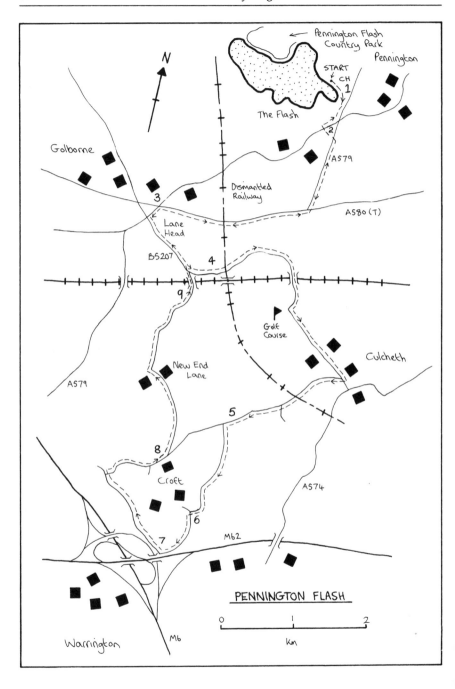

N

Pennington Flash
Country Park

Pennington

START
CH
1

The Flash

2

A579

Golborne

Dismantled
Railway

3

A580 (T)

Lane
Head

B5207

4

9

Golf
Course

Culcheth

New End
Lane

A579

5

A574

8

Croft

6

7

M62

PENNINGTON FLASH

0   1   2

Km

Warrington   M6

right turn into Hob Hey Lane. Go right and ride out of town over the old railway bridge.

5. After about half a mile, look for a turning on the left, signposted to the parish church. This is Lady Lane and it could not be more pleasant, with views across the fields to the spire of Winwick Church. Pass by Croft Church.

6. Turn right into New Lane, then next left after 100 metres into Spring Lane passing stables and towards the M62 motorway. Go right at the T-junction.

7. On reaching a bend keep ahead into Dam Lane, which is narrower and with poor sight lines — so take care. On reaching the next major junction go right into Smithy Brow to ride back into Croft.

8. Pass by the Horseshoe public house and go left as signposted to Lowton by the General Elliott pub. There's a gentle climb up to New Lane End where there's another right turn into The Plough into Kenyon Lane.

9. Joint the B5207 to return to Lane End. All but the suicidal should dismount before the traffic lights and walk up the pavement on the right to re-join the cycleway alongside the A580. Return to Pennington Flash.

Ride 15: Rivington

This ride offers exceptional views of Anglezarke and Rivington reservoirs. It is in two parts, an easy section of 8 miles along back lanes and two off-road sections. For those who enjoy a harder ride (of 10 miles) there is an extension to the upper tip of Anglezarke which includes a 1½ mile section of rough surfaced bridleway.

Start: Visitor Centre, Lever Park, Rivington

Distance: 8 or 10 miles depending on easy or harder option chosen

Map: O.S. Landranger sheet 109 Manchester

Terrain: The 8-mile ride is relatively easy going but the extension is much harder with climbs and descents.

Level of Traffic: Most of the route is off-road, but the roads around Rivington can become busy on summer afternoons.

Rail access: Adlington (Lancashire). There is a link ride to the route from the station using roads. Leave Adlington Railway Station along a minor cobbled road. On reaching Railway Road, turn right and follow this to the centre. Traffic lights ease the passage across the busy A673 road but watch for left turners. Go ahead into Babylon Lane to climb out of Adlington. Join the route at paragraph 4.

Refreshment: Great House Barn Visitor Centre at Lever Park, or at one of the hostelries on route.

Places of Interest:

Lever Park

On a July evening in 1588, a beacon was lit near to where the existing Pike stands, to warn of the advance of the Spanish Armada towards English soil. Not that the Pike or nor the parkland would have existed then. Rivington Pike Tower, by far the best known landmark hereabouts, was built later in the 1730s principally as a folly to mark a boundary. It is almost certain though that it would have been built on a site known from medieval times as a place to signal danger.

Lord Lever, founder of the giant soap company, bought the

parklands and enhanced them considerably at the turn of the 20th century, with the addition of the terraced gardens and several follies, such as the hillside dovecote and waterfront Liverpool Castle. He then donated the park to the public in 1902.The reservoirs were built 50 to 60 years earlier to supply water to West Lancashire towns and Liverpool and still serve a similar purpose.

The Visitor Centre is housed in Great House Barn. This is a reconstructed building, thought originally to date from Saxon times but obviously restored and modified through the ages. The high cruck trusses supporting the roof are a clear indication of their antiquity.

North West Water Cycle Rides

North West Water publish two cycle rides based on the Visitor Centre. Number 1 is a 7½ mile ride around the reservoirs and on bridleways through Lever Park. It is easy going. Number 2 is a far harder climb up to Rivington Pike at 1191 feet. The views are exquisite but make sure that you are up to it. The circuit is only 5 miles in length but strenuous. Neither of the routes are way-marked but they are illustrated on laminated cards.

Rivington

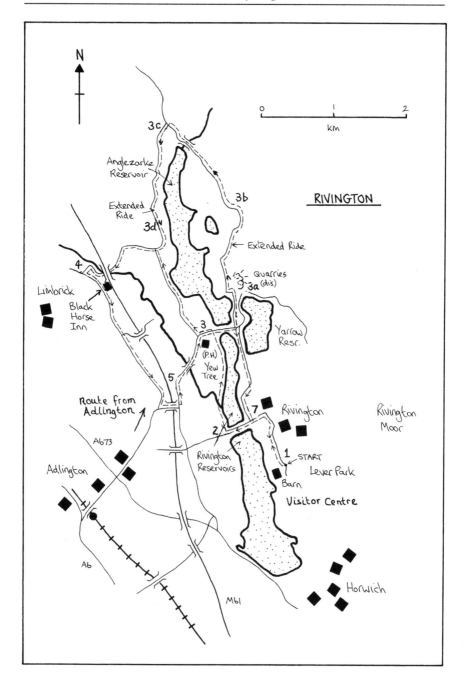

The Route

From the Visitor Centre, Great Barn, Rivington

1. Go left along the road towards Rivington, but cut left along a bridleway which leads slightly left towards the reservoir. This joins another and brings you to a road below Rivington village. Turn left and ride across the bridge.

2. At the other side of the bridge the road rises. Go right by the old lodge along a private road but access is permitted by the landowner. The road is used as a public footpath, but cycles are allowed – please ride with consideration.

3. Exit onto Knowsley Lane and turn left. At the next junction, before the Yew Tree Inn, go right with care. This much quieter road, known appropriately as Back Lane, runs beneath the embankment of Anglezarke reservoir and climbs gently up to Limbrick before dropping beneath the M61 to a junction with the busier Long Lane.

4. Go left to climb up the bank by The Black Horse public house and, a little further up, you pass a butcher's shop. Long Lane begins to feel longer as you climb steadily up to the Bay Horse pub on your right. This is where the road from Adlington enters.

5. Keep left to cross the M61 again and then go left again into Knowsley Lane. Ride past the Yew Tree inn and onward to Anglezarke Reservoir. At the far end of the dam as the road bends left go right to access a bridleway. This climbs up steeply to a junction with a far larger track. Go right.

6. Continue ahead along this popular route with Yarrow reservoir above (and not seen) and Upper Rivington below. You reach a junction with a metalled road. Turn right and the road runs through to the main route used on your outward run.

7. Go left and then right at Rivington Village Green to return to the visitor centre.

The Extended Ride (Hard Going).

3a. Follow the easy route in paragraphs 1 and 2. At point 3, turn right instead of left. Ride across the dam and bear left at the junction. This rises remorselessly up a steep bank by car parks. The view from the top is exceptional. Pass by Jepson's farm where accommodation is available.

3b. A moorland section of road then descends past the Manor House and crosses the feeder canal known as The Goyt at the top end of the reservoir. There is a little more climbing up to Cliffs Farm.

3c. Opposite is a rough bridleway which climbs up the hillside by old quarry workings. You reach a junction where a concessionary bridleway bears right. Keep ahead.

3d. The bridleway continues to a bend where a water authority track runs right down to Back Lane. The bridleway is way-marked ahead. Lift your bike over the step and pass to the right of the farm and buildings. Ride down the drive to Back Lane. Go right to Limbrick, following the remainder of the instructions in paragraph 3 and then through to number 7.

Ride 16: Romiley

An exploration of the Goyt Valley and the interesting corner of Chadkirk. Romiley is congested with traffic, so be careful on the roads in this vicinity.

Start: Romiley Railway Station

Distance: 6 miles

Terrain: Few climbs, easy going for the most part. Half on roads, half on bridleways. Hybrid or Mountain bike preferable.

Level of Traffic: Have to cross the A627 twice which is busy road.

Rail access: Romiley. Daily service from Manchester.

Refreshment: There are several pubs and cafes in Romiley.

Places of Interest:

Chadkirk

Chadkirk chapel, standing by Chadkirk farm, has recently been restored by Stockport Heritage Services. A church was built here in the 7th century by St Chad, the century Bishop of Lichfield who travelled widely, preaching Christianity throughout the land.A small monastic group of clergy settled here, no doubt, to farm the rich pastures lying near to the River Goyt, a pretty river spoilt only by pollution. The existing building dates from the 14th century.

Just after Chadkirk Farm look for a well on the left-hand side. This is also thought to have been associated with St Chad.

Valley Way

The ride joins the Valley Way. This mainly uses public footpaths. The Valley Way also incorporates the Midshires Way so you will see two logos on waymark posts. The idea is eventually to create a route suitable for cyclists, horse riders and walkers but not all sections are geared for all three groups of users yet, especially the section between Compstall and Stockport.

The bridleway section between Middle Farm and Otterspool is particularly attractive. The canopy of trees, grazing pastures and birdsong make it difficult to believe that you are in the heart of an urban area. Only a glance back at the chimney of Pear Mill reminds you that the valley has been the subject of intense industrialisation during the past two centuries.

The Route

1. Descend from the railway station to the main street opposite the Romiley Arms. Cross the main road to ride down Beech Lane. Cross into Urwick Road.

2. Go right into St David's Avenue and left into Green Lane which bends left to run through industrial units before descending to a low tunnel beneath the Peak Forest Canal.

3. At the junction beneath the church take the lower loop to the main A627 known as Hatherlow here. Cross into Overdale Road. Go next right into The Ridgeway. Follow this around until it meets Bredbury Green.

4. Turn left to pass by schools. Turn next left down Highfield Avenue. This bends right and left into Highfield Avenue. Continue ahead down Shakespeare Road until it gives out to an opening and Vernon Woods.

5. Cycle through the wood to cross a bridge then go left to descend to a crossroads by the entrance to Bredbury Hall. Go left.

6. The bridleway runs into the Goyt Valley. It bends left and runs through the farmyard of Middle Farm. Be considerate as you ride through. It then passes to the left of Goyt Hall.

7. You come to a junction where the Valley Way is signposted right to Stockport and ahead for Chadkirk. The path on the right is not suitable for cycling but offers a short walk to a beauty spot where a bridge spans the River Goyt.

8. Continue ahead on the bridleway to pass Waterside Farm on the left and a kennels on the right. You emerge at the A627 at Otterspool Bridge. Cross the road here and wheel your bike along the pavement ahead.

9. Go right along Vale Road to Chadkirk Farm. The road winds up the hillside, under the canal and back into Romiley.

10. Ride up Chadkirk Road. Turn right, back into Beech Lane.

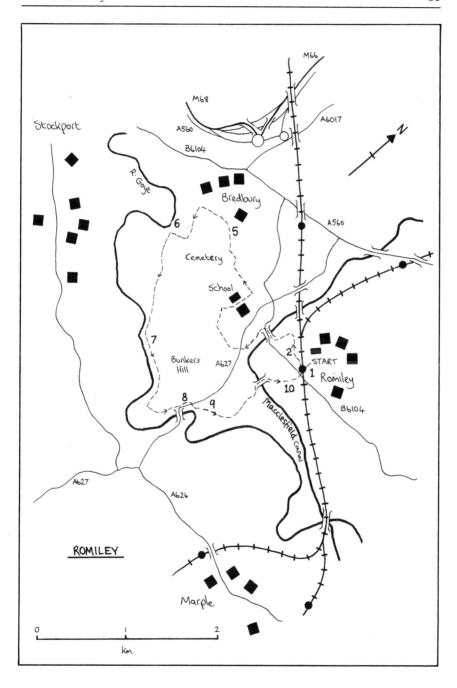

Ride 17: Stalybridge

*An easy ride along the Staley Way and up to the reservoir at
Brushes. Those venturing further will discover some of the tops
above Mossley.*

Start: Mottram Road Car Park, Stalybridge

Distance: 5 miles easy short route, with hard extension 11 miles

Map: O.S. Landranger 109 Manchester

Terrain: The Staley Way is an easy ride and there follows a gradual climb up to
Brushes where there is an option to return. Most will cope with this.
Those who like hard climbs should continue as the 6 mile extension to Mossley Brow
offers steeper hills. A hybrid or mountain bike is essential for this.

Level of Traffic: Quiet except crossing the B6175. The extension involves a run
through Mossley and a short section of the busy A670, otherwise it follows quiet lanes.

Rail access: Stalybridge station is half a mile from Mottram Road on busy roads.

Refreshment: At Brushes and Mossley there are several pubs, plus the very pleasant
Hare and Hounds at Luzley.

Places of Interest:

Brushes

The reservoir and country park here have been developed in recent
years as part of an on-going programme to improve recreational
access in the Tame Valley.

Mossley

As mentioned in Ride 11, Mossley is in many respects three separate
communities. These reflect the earlier growth of dwellings and
commerce which occurred in three different counties. The extremely hard climb up from Mossley Railway Station to Mossley
Brow is a prime example.

Luzley

This ancient hamlet is one of the most isolated parts of Greater Manchester. The views across the conurbation are exquisite.

The Route

1. Leave the car park by way of the barrier. A narrow path curves to the main cycle route. Go right and follow this until a short sharp descent to Grove Road.

2. Go right up Grove Road to Brushes. Cross the main road by the Royal Oak and enter Stalybridge Country Park where there is a small green visitor centre built in the style of a fortress.

3. The bridleway passes to the right of it and climbs behind houses to a junction. Go left as signposted to Walkerwood Reservoir.

4. This runs through scrub to exit onto a road. Go left to ride along the dam, with fine views of the reservoir and the country park below.

5. At the end of the reservoir you can cycle for a short distance up the valley, using the road to the right. Otherwise go left along an unmade road towards Millbrook. Those returning should go left down Besom Lane back to the main road and The Royal Oak. Retrace your wheels back to Stalybridge.

Extension

6. Those seeking the harder climb extension should turn right and begin to cycle uphill. It climbs through a fold known as Sub Green, bending right and then left to rise up to the isolated scattering of houses of Hyde Green. The rough track then continues ahead to descend to a mill.

7. Go left and follow the perimeter of the mill down to a junction. Keep ahead and then join Beaconsfield Terrace. The road becomes Thorny Lane and the Castle Lane. There's a hard climb up to Castle Farm.

8. The road looks as if it bends right up to the quarry but your way is ahead to the right of the farm. You pass Micklehurst Cricket Club. Then, drop steeply to the B6175.

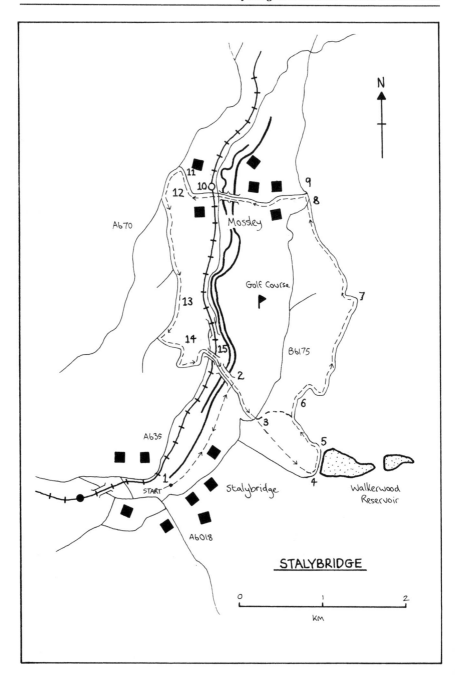

N

A670

11
10
12
Mossley
8
9

Golf Course

13

7

14
15
B6175

2

A635

6

3

5

4

START
1
Stalybridge
Walkerwood
Reservoir

A6018

STALYBRIDGE

0   1   2
Km

9. Go right and around the corner turn left into Micklehurst Road. This drops down to the canal and climbs up to the main road. It is better to dismount and walk up Mill Street (one way road) to Mossley Railway Station.

10. Ride up Stamford Road but as it bends right go ahead up Old Brow. At the top bear right and then left into Vale Street and then right into Old Brow again, a formidable climb.

11. Pass by the unusual looking Highland Laddie pub and then turn left along Wyre Street and left again into Upper Mossley's square.

12. Go left on the main road to rise out of the town. Be careful not to miss the left turning, Luzley Lane. This rises to a brow and descends to the hamlet of Luzley. Bear left at the junction by The Hare and Hounds pub.

13. The road descends – be warned that you will soon come to a very uneven surface of setts. This old road drops to a junction of dirt tracks.

14. Go left along Spout Brook which can become a torrent in inclement weather. The lane winds its way down to houses in Heyrod.

15. At the main Wakefield road (by The Grapes Hotel) dismount to cross the road and walk to the left for 50 metres to Spring Bank on the right. It drops to the canal and then return on the Staley Way to your starting point.

Ride 18: Stockport

An easy ride along disused railway tracks which provide an excellent starter for those who seek traffic free cycling and no hills.

Start: Car park on Tiviot Way.

Distance: 6 miles

Map: O.S. Landranger map 109 Manchester

Terrain: Cycle ways: few gradients and one descent.

Level of Traffic: Only one short section of quiet road

Rail access: Stockport railway station is one mile away but the route across town is not recommended as the traffic factor is high.

Refreshment: Pubs and cafes in Stockport

Places of Interest:

Reddish Vale

This route is similar to that described in the Greater Manchester Bike Rides – Reddish Vale. Part of the route has also been incorporated into the Trans Pennine Trail. The Reddish Vale Visitor Centre lies at the heart of an old calico printing mill, which printed patterns onto plain white or bleached cotton cloth. The pools (or lodges) are now home to a range of wildfowl, including two favourites with children: the Great Crested Glebe and Tufted Duck.

You might also like to see the exhibitions about Reddish Vale or stop off for a picnic while you watch the trains pass by on the viaduct which towers above the bubbling waters of the River Tame.

Brinnington Tunnel

The tunnel was opened in January 1863, a vital link in opening the Stockport to Woodley railway via Portwood, a quiet section of railway which closed in recent decades. It is one of the many small link lines which existed in Manchester until recent times. Thankfully it has been safeguarded for recreational use, rather than being absorbed into the road network.

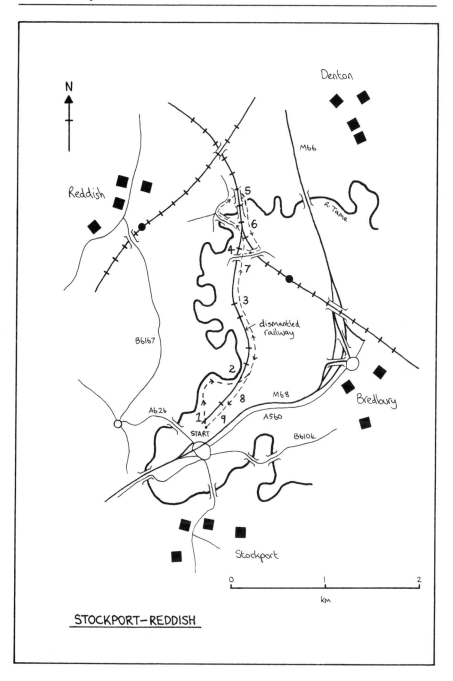

STOCKPORT-REDDISH

The Route

1. From the entrance to the car park, take the route on the left which passes two barriers and then skirts the River Tame. Follow this through the park to a bridge.

2. Do not cross it but instead bear right to climb the bank. It comes to a junction with the main cycle route utilising the disused railway, once known as The Deadline. Go left.

3. The route continues along the hillside of Reddish Vale. To the left is Reddish Vale Golf Course. The trail rises to double gates and an access road to the golf course.

4. Your way is slightly left along a narrow metalled path signposted to Reddish Vale Visitor Centre. This drops steeply into the valley, so apply brakes before descending. It comes to a junction and flower meadow. Go left for the Visitor Centre.

5. Return to the meadow but this time keep left to ride beneath the impressive Reddish Viaduct. The cycle path then bears right to a barrier at the bank.

6. The path climbs and you bear right to continue up the bluff. This is difficult to ride but once at the top a narrow route runs ahead then left to exit by houses at Blackberry Lane. Go right and right again until it reaches the access point mentioned in Paragraph 4.

7. Retrace your wheels back towards Stockport. Go ahead at the junction where you joined previously but at the next junction bear left up to join the Valley Way route.

8. Go right for the car park. You might like to go left to ride through the Brinnington Tunnel and through to a meadow above the M63. There's a good view of 20th century transport from here.

9. There's no viable circular route without encountering heavy traffic, so retrace your wheels back to Stockport.

Ride 19: Tandle Hill

An easy ride along lanes which have fortunately fallen from being major thoroughfares to unsurfaced lanes, where the car is excluded. Hopefully, it will remain this way.

Start: Tandle Hill Country Park

Distance: 5 miles

Map: O.S. Landranger 109 Manchester

Terrain: Easy Going. Rough surfaces. Hybrid or Mountain bike preferable.

Level of Traffic: Very quiet except for short section on A671.

Rail access: None

Refreshment: There's a cafe at Tandle Hill Country Park and the Tandle Hill public house at Thornham Fold.

Places of Interest:

Tandle Hill Country Park

Donated to the people of Oldham by Norris Bradbury in 1919, Tandle Hill is a joy to walk but ironically cycles are not welcome and there are notices to this effect at most entrances. It is primarily known for its extensive beech woodland; in recent times, fir cone sculptures have become a point of interest in the park. The name Tandle refers to fire; in the early 1800s, it was the site of many stormy political meetings which led to the Peterloo Massacre at St Peter's Field in Manchester.

Oldham

Oldham was a major centre of cotton manufacturing before the turn of the last century. There were well over 300 five-storey mills in the area. The peak of production was most probably in the 1890s although this might well have extended to the First World War when cotton manufacture began to decline noticeably.

Oldham is known now for its shopping and markets, but the

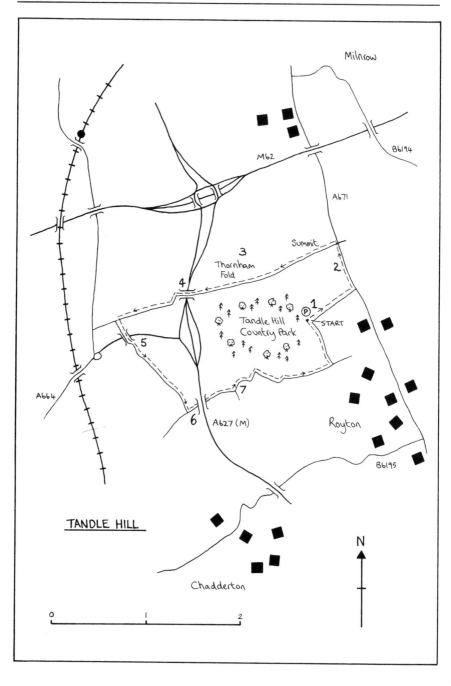

Milnrow

B6194

M62

A671

3

Summit

Thornham
Fold

2

4

1

Tandle Hill
Country Park

(P)

START

5

7

6   A627 (M)

Royton

A664

B6195

TANDLE HILL

N

Chadderton

0   1   2

Borough is continually seeking to improve access to the countryside, including cycle routes in recent times. There is a very useful town trail leaflet as walking is far easier than cycling in central Oldham.

The Route

1. From the car park at Tandle Hill Country Park, ride back to the main A671 road. Turn left to climb the hill to Summit.

2. Descend to a crossroads where you turn left opposite Thornham Lane. This is Thornham Old Road, which runs along the edge of the Country Park.

3. Pass through Thornham Fold, consisting of just a farm and the Tandle Hill public house.

4. The ride crosses over the motorway and bends left and right down to Slattocks, passing a school on your right. At the turning to the church go left at Toll Bar Cottage.

5. This old road joins Stakehill Lane, by an industrial estate. Go left and follow the lane until it comes to a junction at Upper Stakehill.

6. Turn left by the row of terraces and the track bears left and right to go under the motorway. It then rises slightly to a junction. Keep ahead.

7. Ride with care through the farmyard at Hough then continue along Oozewood Road until you reach a metalled road. Go left into Tandle Park Road which rises up to Tandle Hill Road. Go left for the country park.

Ride 20: Whaley Bridge

A hard ride which is packed with climbs, descents and magnificent views in this wilder part of the Goyt Valley. Only for those who like a challenge.

Start: Whaley Bridge railway station

Distance: 12 miles

Map: O.S. Landranger Sheets 110 Sheffield and Huddersfield and 119 Buxton, Matlock and Dove Dale.

Terrain: Very hilly

Level of Traffic: Very little except for Whaley Bridge.

Rail access: Whaley Bridge

Refreshment: Whaley Bridge, Combs and Buxworth

Places of Interest:

Buxworth

The Navigation, which stands by the inland port of Buxworth, is a good place to stop for refreshment and you can muse here on the village name. It has always been something of a contention. It most probably derives from a Ralph Bugge, a bailiff of the Peak Forest in the mid 13th century. Little did he know that it would lead to ridicule and eventually to the changing of the name Bugsworth to Buxworth. It was in the late 1920s that the local clergyman led parishioners to petition Parliament for a change of name. With much amazement, Parliament granted permission for the change but the story ran for months in *Punch* magazine, so good was the yarn.

 The restored wharves illustrate what an important trans-shipment centre this must have been in the early 1800s, with space for up to 20 narrow boats.

Combs

Riding above the valley on your way into Combs you might catch a glimpse of Tunstead farm below, reckoned to be haunted by "Tunstead Dicky". This unfortunate farmer, on returning from the Napoleonic Wars, was enraged to find that his cousin had not only taken his farm but also his wife. The cousin was also sharp with rage and chopped off poor Dicky's head. It is said that from that day onwards the skull of Dicky reappeared at the farm repeatedly. Only when placed in the farmhouse did the spirit lay to rest and it is said that it remains there to this day.

The beginnings of the Ferodo business started in Combs, no doubt at the Beehive pub, when Bert Froode invented brake shoes. Having observed how local farmers were accustomed to using old boots to extend the life of the crude brake blocks of their farm machinery, Froode started what has since become the Ferodo business ("Ferodo" being an anagram of his name). On the other side of the railway embankment is Combs reservoir, which is an extremely popular haunt for walkers and sailors.

Eccles Pike

This high ground, now administered by the National Trust, was once a place where locals gathered to light a bonfire if there was rumour of invasion.

Whaley Bridge

Whaley Bridge has changed much during the past 10 years from a sleepy old town to something of a bustling visitor centre for the area. There are now cafes and antique shops where meat and veg were once sold. In earlier times Whaley was a major trans-shipment centre for goods between the Peak Forest Canal and the Cromford and High Peak Railway, which was built in the 1830s. The incline through Whaley Bridge can still be seen.

The Route

1. From the railway station in Whaley Bridge go left and then immediately right into the high street. Pass by the White Hart public house on the left and turn next left, but not immediately left, into Old Road.

2. This climbs through the town to rejoin the main Manchester

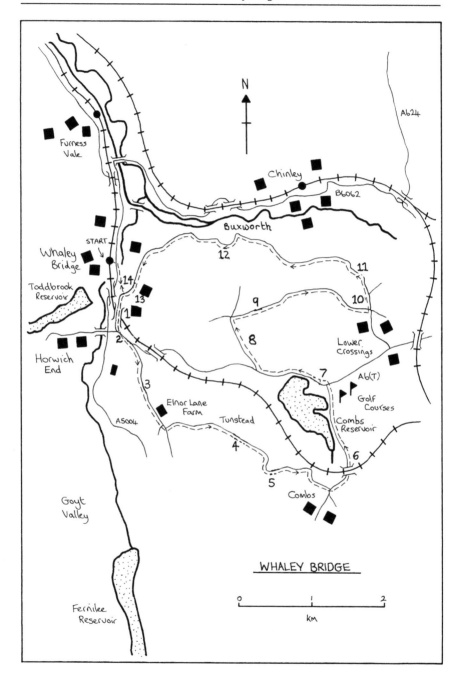

N

A624

Furness
Vale

Chinley

B6062

Buxworth

START

12

11

Whaley
Bridge

Toddbrook
Reservoir

14

10

13

9

1

8

2

Lower
Crossings

Horwich
End

7

A6(T)

3

Golf
Courses

Elnor Lane
Farm

Combs
Reservoir

A5004

Tunstead

4

6

5

Goyt
Valley

Combs

Fernilee
Reservoir

WHALEY BRIDGE

0   1   2

km

Road. Turn left and ride along the main road. You will see the Board Inn on the left and a bus shelter and stop on the right. Make the right turn here into Elnor Lane.

3. This rises remorselessly up through Shallcross. At the top of the housing go left at the fork. The road continues to rise past Elnor Farm, where there are all sorts of animals to see. Just beyond the farm turn left along an unsurfaced track, known as Long Lane but not marked in any way.

4. This exceptional lane offers a chance to enjoy a mile off-road but you might still meet motor cycles and the occasional vehicle. The views across Combs Reservoir are exquisite. Long Lane drops from Ladder Hill to a junction below Thorny Lee Farm.

5. Go left and check your speed as the descent is quite steep as you pass Spire Hollins. Enter the hamlet of Combs and go left by the Beehive pub.

6. The road runs beneath the railway bridge and then alongside Combs reservoir where parked cars can be a nuisance at busy times. On reaching the main B5470 road turn left for a half mile ride to Milton Tunstead.

7. You will see the Rose and Crown pub on the right to the right. Turn next right at the end of the houses. The sight line is better than you first imagine but, if in doubt, dismount.

8. The lane up to Eccles Pike is narrow and steep but the views up top make the sweat worthwhile. You'll probably have to walk some stretches and be warned-this section of road gets icy in winter.

9. Rise up to a junction and turn right. The climbing continues until you reach the summit of Eccles Pike. Then, prepare for a steep descent to the main road at Higher Crossings.

10. Turn left. The road dips and rises before a long descent to Chinley. Look for a turning on the left in approximately a quarter of a mile, which is not signposted.

11. This narrow lane runs by Eccles House and Fold before descending steeply. It then rises to a junction. Bear right and

free-wheel down to Buxworth, along Western Lane where there are many parked cars.

12. At the junction go right for the Basin. Otherwise turn left along an unsigned road which is narrow and steep. Frogs and toads migrate annually to this steep section.

13. The road levels and dips to run into the outskirts of Whaley Bridge. It then falls far more steeply as Bings Road to join Old Road.

14. Turn right to return to the centre of Whaley Bridge but be wary at the right-hand turn in the centre.

Cyclists' Directory

This chapter is packed with useful contact addresses, telephone numbers and snippets of information regarding cycle hire, holidays, cycle shops and campaigning organisations.

Useful Organisations

British Waterways

In recent years British Waterways has changed its policy towards cycling on canal-side tow-paths. Some sections have been opened to cyclists where local Waterway managers feel the need to encourage the use of tow-paths. The mileage is not large and there is still no general public right of way for cyclists on all tow-paths.

If you would like to ride on the sections that are eligible then you have to apply for a tow-path permit (which is free of charge) and agree to observe a common sense safety code. You need to display the permit on your bike when cycling the tow-paths. British Waterways are not being mean about this. They simply argue that many tow-paths are currently not in a good condition for cycling or are too narrow for safe riding. The Black Country Cycleway in the West Midlands and the Leeds and Liverpool Canal show what can be done when British Waterways and local authorities join together to improve tow-paths for all users.

Sections available for cycling in and around Greater Manchester are as follows:

Leeds and Liverpool Canal

Burscough (Bridge 32A) through Wigan to Springs Bridge (59A)

Sennicar (Bridge 61) to White Bear, Adlington (Bridge 69)

Most of the remainder of the Leeds and Liverpool canal across the Pennines is available to cyclists and makes for a great short break holiday.

Peak Forest Canal
The Marple Flight of locks only.

Ashton Canal
Ducie Street Basin to Portland Basin

Contact Telephone Numbers:
Pennine and Potteries Waterways
Top Lock
Church Lane
Marple
Cheshire SK6 6BN. Tel: 0160 427 1079

Leeds and Liverpool Canal (West)
Aldercliffe Road
Lancaster
LA1 1SU. Tel: (01524) 32712

If you have general enquiries about cycling elsewhere in the country 'phone British Waterways Customer Service at Watford on (01923) 226422

Please note that the Bridgewater Canal Company does not allow cycling on the Bridgewater Canal, nor can you cycle alongside the Manchester Ship Canal.

Cycling Organisations

Cycling Project for the North West (CPNW)

In Manchester the key organisation to contact is CPNW, based at the Environmental Institute, Bolton Road, Swinton, Manchester M27 2UX. Tel: (0161) 794 1926.

CPNW is a registered charity whose main aim is to promote cycling in the North West. It shares offices with several organisations at the Institute (which is just off the Bolton Road) and there you can buy leaflets and booklets on cycling, or simply call in to seek advice on cycling routes. If you are travelling some distance it might be best to call to ensure that someone is at the office.

The way to get the best out of CPNW and to support its good work is to join its membership scheme for a small sum. CPNW has produced a fold-out leaflet and map "Cycling In The North West" which you will find very useful when travelling around the region.

There is also a series of cycle ride leaflets "Bike Rides in Greater Manchester" as follows:

1: Sale Water Park

2: Reddish Vale

3. Dunham Town Circular

4. Saddleworth Circular

5. Watling Street

6. Hartshead Pike

7. The Salford Loop Lines

A small charge is made for each leaflet.

Cyclists' Touring Club (known as the CTC)
Cotterell House
69 Meadrow
Godalming
Surrey GU7 3HS. Tel: (01483) 417217

This is Britain's largest national cycling club, with approximately 40,000 members. Membership of the CTC includes many services

Cycling near Dunham Massey

such as insurance and legal aid, a bi-monthly magazine, handbook, technical and touring advice, mail order and shop service. The CTC also provides guided cycling holidays in the UK and around the world.

It also gets involved in important campaigning matters such as the provision of cycle facilities in towns but is also greatly concerned about cycle touring in the countryside. For example, it has spear-headed in recent times a campaign to save country lanes which it rightly describes as "one of the glories of the British Isles. "The second threat is development, especially on the urban fringes. New housing estates, out of town shopping areas and industrial estates stimulate a demand for enhancements to existing road networks. Local lanes often become incorporated into such improvement schemes with a loss of amenity. The CTC really do need our help with campaigns such as this. It is worthwhile joining simply to back these. Head Office will supply details of up to date contact addresses in Greater Manchester.

Sustrans

Sustrans is a legend in its own right. Within the last decade it has done so much to bring cycling back to the agenda of transport issues. It has illustrated the way in which local authorities can stimulate a considerable shift from car to bike for local journeys by building off-road routes. For example, the Bristol to Bath cycle path carries well over a million cycle trips per annum, or nearly 3,000 journeys per day.

Sustrans provide advice and consultancy on the design and building of such routes across the land. It has a major campaign to build a national cycle network of at least 5,000 miles using disused railway lines, canal tow-paths, riversides and derelict land in part-nership with other organisations. Like the CTC it is also keen to see traffic calmed country roads so that we can enjoy the very best of the countryside without the fear of traffic. Sustrans is, without doubt, at the leading edge of cycle provision and equally deserves our support. They can be contacted at: 35 King St, Bristol, BS1 4DZ. Tel: (0117) 929 0888.

Useful Facilities

Useful facilities for cyclists in and around Greater Manchester are as follows:

Cycle Hire

Mid and North Cheshire

Bollington
Groundwork Macclesfield and Vale Royal, Adelphi Mill Gate Lodge, Grimshaw Lane Tel: (01625) 572681

Delamere Forest
Discovery Centre, Linmere. For telephone contact, see Bollington entry.

Tatton Park
For telephone contact, see Bollington entry

North West Derbyshire

Buxton
Mountain Bike Experience, 6 New Cottages Tel: (01298) 71674

Hayfield
Buckingham's Mountain Bikes, Royal Hotel Tel: (0161) 477 7346 or Mobile: (0831) 196209
Derbyshire County Council Cycle Hire, Information Centre, Station Road, Hayfield Tel: (01663) 746222

Whaley Bridge
Peak District MTB Centre, 3 Market St Tel: (01663) 735020

Greater Manchester

Horwich
Bolton Mountain Bikes, Car Park, Lever Park Tel: (01204) 847758 or (0831) 132590
D Tours, 49 Hope St, Horwich Tel: (01204) 699460

Offerton
Bednall Cycle Hire, 16 Salcombe Road Tel: (0161) 477 4493

South Lancashire

Clitheroe
Pedal Power Mountain Bike Hire, Waddington Road Tel: (01200) 22066

Whalley
Adult Education Centre, Station Road Tel: (01254) 822717

Cycle Holidays

Freewheel Cycle Tours, Clitheroe. Tel: (01200) 442069. Self-guided tours available in Lancashire and Yorkshire.
Two North West based companies offering holidays in France are
Headwater, Northwich, Cheshire CW9 5BR Tel (01606) 42220
Susi Madron's Cycling For Softies, 2 & 4 Birch Polygon, Manchester M14 5HX Tel (0161) 248 8282

Cycle Shops

Bolton
Bolton Mountain Bikes, 247, Blackburn Road, Egerton. Tel: (01204) 594418
Green Machine Bike Shop, 142 Lee Lane, Horwich. Tel: (01204) 696831
Parkers of Bolton, Shiffnall House, Shiffnall Street. Tel: (01204) 531323
Geoff Smith, 229 St. Helens Road. Tel: (01204) 653509

Bury
E.B. Cycles, 305 Bolton Rd. Tel: (0161) 763 6110
Pilkington Cycles, 101 The Rock. Tel: (0161) 764 2723
Riggi Cycle Sport, 48 Moorgate. Tel: (0161) 797 3259

Cheadle
Discount Cycles, 249 Stockport Rd. Tel: (0161) 428 3311
Meadows, 5 Gatley Rd. Tel: (0161) 428 6596
Morris, 4 Borden Rd, Cheadle Heath. Tel: (0161) 480 5520

Eccles
Brooks Ltd, 32 Liverpool Rd, Eccles. Tel: (0161) 789 1336
Metro Cycles, 410 Liverpool Rd, Eccles. Tel: (0161) 707 1333

Hazel Grove
Brookes Cycles, The Boulevard, Chester Rd. Tel: (0161) 483 2261
H&C Cycles, 86 Commercial Rd. Tel: (0161) 483 2819

Handforth
Rick Green Cycles, 61 Wilmslow Rd. Tel: (01625) 532325

Heywood
Ron's Cycles, 52a Manchester St. Tel: (01706) 622603
Shepherds Cycles, 45 Market St. Tel: (01706) 360305

Hyde
Oldham Cycles, 175 Market St. Tel: (0161) 368 1749

Littleborough
Gale Cycles, 1 Hollingworth Rd. Tel (01706) 374482

Manchester
A1 Cycle Centre, 414 Palatine Road, Northenden. Tel: (0161) 998 2882
Bardsley, 482 Manchester Rd, Heaton Chapel. Tel: (0161) 432 4936
Bicycle Doctor, 70 Dickenson Road, Rusholme. Tel: (0161) 224 1303
Bikehouse, 177 School Lane. Tel: (0161) 443 1235
Crown Point Cycles, 50 Stockport Rd. Tel: (0161) 336 8138
Cycle-Ops, 219 Droylsden Rd, Audenshaw. Tel: (0161) 370 1847
Derby Shop, 119 Liverpool Rd, Cadishead. Tel: (0161) 775 3864
Forsters Cycle Centre, 376 Barlow Moor Rd, Chorlton. Tel: (0161) 881 7160
Freewheel, 190 Deansgate. Tel: (0161) 832 3444
Harry Hall Cycles, 31 Corn Exchange, Hanging Ditch. Tel: (0161) 832 1369
Heaton Park Cycle Depot, 227 Bury Rd, Prestwich. Tel: (0161) 773 4977
Johns Cycles, 38a High Lane. Tel: (0161) 861 0984
Moston Cycles, 372 Moston Lane, Moston. Tel: (0161) 681 0945
Northend, 2 Lime Grove, Denton. Tel: (0161) 336 4142
On Your Bike, 166 Deansgate. Tel: (0161) 839 6011

Orrell, 395 Hollinwood Avenue, New Moston. Tel: (0161) 681 1517

Pedal Power, 61 Crumpsall Lane. Tel: (0161) 795 4388

Rowbothams, 470 Oldham Rd, Failsworth. Tel: (0161) 681 1671

Timperley Cycles, 208 Stockport Rd. Tel: (0161) 980 3069

Threadgold, 189 Hollyhedge Rd. Tel: (0161) 998 2287

U-Go Cycles, 117 Princess Rd, Mosside. Tel: (0161) 227 9474

Walton Cycles, 8 Warburton St, Didsbury. Tel: (0161) 446 2084

Withington Cycles, 26 Burton Rd, Withington. Tel: (0161) 445 3492

Marple

Marple Cycle Sport, 138 Stockport Rd. Tel: (0161) 427 5551

Middleton

Middleton Cycles, 70 Long St. Tel: (0161) 653 5937

Morton Pitts Cycles, 434 Oldham Rd, Middleton. Tel: (0161) 643 4159

Mossley

Mossley Cycles, 12 Manchester Rd. Tel: (01457) 835913

Oldham

Astleys, 298 Heron St. Tel: (0161) 624 1478

Oldham Cycle Centre, 87 Lees Rd. Tel: (0161) 624 8260

SHD Cycles, 147 Ashton Rd. Tel: (0161) 620 4319

The Bike Shop, Rosedale Shopping Centre, Old Church St. Tel: (0161) 681 6001

Shaw and Crompton Cycles, 7 Button Hole, Shaw. Tel: (01706) 847550

Skidmores, 37 Union St. Tel: (0161) 624 5912

Suntal, 45 Ripponden Rd. Tel: (0161) 624 7409

Radcliffe

Geoff Hayes, 80 Water St. Tel: (0161) 723 2807

Rochdale

Cycle Save, 61 Market St, Whitworth. Tel: (01706) 57162

Kingsway Bikes, 240 Oldham Rd. Tel: (01706) 46686

Paulson Cycles, 246 Yorkshire St. Tel: (01706) 33426

Sale

Devereux Cycles, 45 Green Lane. Tel: (0161) 973 5234

Salford
Freds Auto Cycles, 55 Tootal Rd, Salford. Tel: (0161) 736 5080

Stalybridge
Bridge Cycles, 85 Market St. Tel: (0161) 338 7644

Stockport
Morris, 9 Offerton Drive, Offerton. Tel: (0161) 483 5132
Thorpe's Cycles, 1 Wellington Rd. Tel: (0161) 480 3992
Woodsons Cycles, 85 Castle St. Tel: (0161) 480 8725

Urmston
Manchester Cycle Exchange, 1 Brook Terrace. Tel: (0161) 748 2532
Shields Cycles, 1 Old Rd, Failsworth. Tel: (0161) 624 5912

Whitefield
Cooksons Cycles, 195 Bury New Rd. Tel: (0161) 766 2633

Wigan
Bewleys Cycle Store, Shevington. Tel: (01257) 252805

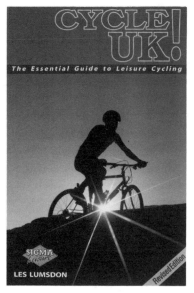